# DAUGHTERS OF ZION

# Daughters Of Zion

### Stories of Old Testament Women
### by
### Elizabeth Watson

FRIENDS
UNITED
PRESS

RICHMOND
INDIANA

Copyright 1982 Friends United Press
  101 Quaker Hill Drive, Richmond, IN 47374
Library of Congress Card Catalog Number 82-70600
ISBN 0-913408-79-4

For my granddaughters —
   Heide, Margaret, Susannah,
      Lara, Svea-Rose and Silke-Mary,
         and Lorelei, born while this
            manuscript was in preparation —
that they go right forward.

*Sing aloud, O daughter of Zion;*
  *shout, O Israel!*
*Rejoice and exult with all your heart,*
  *O daughter of Jerusalem!*

. . . . . . . . . . . . . . . . . . . . . . .

*"I will remove disaster from you,*
  *so that you will not bear reproach for it.*
*Behold, at that time I will deal with all your oppressors.*
*And I will save the lame*
  *and gather the outcast,*
*and I will change their shame into praise*
  *and renown in all the earth.*
*At that time I will bring you home,*
  *at the time when I gather you together;*
*yea, I will make you renowned and praised*
  *among all the peoples of the earth,*
*when I restore your fortunes before your eyes."*

*[Zephaniah 3:14, 18-20]*

# CONTENTS

# Preface

*I, chanter of pains and joys, uniter of here and here-*
*    after,*
*Taking all hints to use them, but swiftly leaping*
*    beyond them,*
*A reminiscence sing.*

Walt Whitman

During most of a long life I have been a Bible reader. I had a
call to the ministry as a child, and I began to prepare for my
calling early. At that time I read the Bible quite literally. As a
teen-ager I read it developmentally, seeing it as the record of
the growth of the Judeo-Christian concept of God from a tribal
divinity of wrath to the God of love and forgiveness. In semi-
nary, nearly half a century ago, we were "demythologizing"
the Bible; more recently I've been "remythologizing" it.
Always I have read it meditatively, finding courage and comfort in its great passages.

In the last dozen years I have been reading the Bible with
still a different approach. I have been searching for and laying
claim to my heritage as a woman in the Judeo-Christian tradition. The Bible is concerned with a masculine God. It was
written by men, translated by men, and, most of the time, inter-
preted by men. Reading with sensitive eyes, however, I have
found many feminine images of God; I have glimpsed a larger
God, one not limited by human concepts of sexuality. I have
been excited to find my spiritual foremothers — women of
incredible courage, capability, coping-skills, and caring.

In the summer of 1980 I was asked to give the Bible half-
hours for the triennial meeting of the United Society of Friends
Women. All that year they had been using a study guide called
*And the Woman Said . . .* , and I welcomed the opportunity to
share some of my special women.

I chose three related stories, *Sarah, Rebekah,* and *Rachel,*
and hoped I could bring them to life. For months beforehand I
had read and reread their stories in different translations and
tried to see events through their eyes, not their husbands' or
God's eyes. I thought at first to tell *about* them, but as the
weeks went on, they wanted to speak for themselves. I let

them. Their stories are filtered through my experience, however, so I have not limited them to a vocabulary appropriate to women four thousand years ago. I have let them comment on my own twentieth century concerns because they were indeed throwing new light on them. I have allowed anachronisms to stand when they crept in, and I have permitted the women to quote passages of scripture that appear at a later time in the Bible, for just as they became part of my life, so I, in turn, became part of theirs.

The stories of Sarah, Rebekah, and Rachel are told quite fully in the Bible, and for them the Bible was virtually my only source. I tried not to contradict the Biblical stories, but I did add details. I permitted reconciliations to take place which the women seemed to desire: Rebekah with Esau, and Rachel with Leah. I did not feel Sarah and Hagar were reconciled, although I think they both wanted to be.

Sarah, Rebekah, and Rachel found their way into a pamphlet called *Let Their Lives Speak,* published by Friends United Press, in June, 1981. The response was sufficient that the Press encouraged me to add more stories and make a larger volume. Nine women appear here now. It was hard to choose, and already I am thinking ahead to a second volume.

With these new stories, the Biblical details are much scantier. I have read widely in commentaries and history for background, and have created the stories in great part from my imagination, trying to find plausible motivations for what the women did.

Lot's Wife appeared in part, in the third person, in the keynote address at New England Yearly Meeting of Friends in August, 1980. Tamar, Rahab, Ruth, and Bathsheba were the Bible half-hours at North Carolina Yearly Meeting (FUM) in 1981.

I am indebted to many people for helpful suggestions and provocative ideas, among them:
— twenty-five women and two brave men who came to a weekend on "Women in the Bible/Women Today" at Powell House, Old Chatham, New York, in November, 1979. The men cheerfully entered into "dancing Sarah's circle" and speaking of the "sisterhood of humankind" for the weekend.
— many women at the United Society of Friends Women Triennial in June, 1980, who took Sarah, Rebekah, and Rachel

to their hearts, and whose response helped me breathe life into them.

— thirty women who joined a workshop on "Women in the Bible" at the Gathering of Friends General Conference in July, 1980. Their imaginations were particularly caught by Lot's wife and Miriam and many of their ideas are included here.

— Jeanne and Wendell Clepper of the Friends Community of North Easton, where I live, who shared with me a paper by Moses Bailey entitled *Imagining How it Was,* in which he mentioned the women included in the genealogy of Jesus which opens Matthew's Gospel. Unfortunately Wendell did not live to see the completed stories which his sharing set in motion.

— Moses Bailey who wrote in his paper: "Into [four] patriarchal beds crept Tamar the Forbidden, Rahab the Prostitute, Ruth the Poor Relation, Bathsheba the Striptease . . . ." I had been looking for four related stories to tell in the Bible half-hours at North Carolina Yearly Meeting, and with his statement I knew that I had found my four women. When I read the details of their stories in the Old Testament, I was not sure North Carolina Friends would welcome them, or me. But they did!

— Rosalind Cobb of the Friends Community at North Easton whose remarkable sculpture portrait entitled "Lot's Wife" fired my imagination. I am indebted to Rosalind for many helpful suggestions about Lot's Wife, who is very real to her, as she is to me. Lot's Wife, in sculpture and story, went together to New England Yearly Meeting.

— Rosalind Cobb and Joan Hepburn of Providence, Rhode Island, for help in brainstorming Miriam, particularly the enigmatic passage about the Cushite wife of Moses. Both are widely read in African history and culture.

— Kara Cole, Administrative Secretary of Friends United Meeting, and acting Editor of Friends United Press at the time *Let Their Lives Speak* was in process, for encouragement, patience, and for deep friendship. We are sisters of the spirit.

— Barbara Hollingsworth, now Editor of Friends United Press, for stretching deadlines, for encouragement, for sharing deeply in a workshop on "Quaker Women and the World" at the Friends General Conference Gathering in Berea in 1981, and for deep friendship. We too are sisters of the spirit.

xiv

— and finally George Watson, never a male chauvanist, who
has cheerfully opened his heart to my Biblical sisters, lived
with them day in and day out, and who has offered many helpful suggestions, as well as vetoing many ideas of mine which
he thought too far-out. His constant editing of the stories as
they took shape was invaluable, even when it hurt.

Eliza Armstrong Cox, founding president of the United
Society of Friends Women a century ago, said, "What shall the
present generation of our women do? *Go right forward . . . .*"

"Go right forward" was the theme of the USFW Triennial in
1980, and Sarah, Rebekah, and Rachel all responded to it.
Those words have kept me at the typewriter to complete this
volume. They are good words for women of all generations.

Elizabeth Watson
North Easton, Massachusetts
December 1981

# Introduction

Sarah and Abraham may have started their long journey from Ur to Canaan about 1980 B.C. They lived in the Middle Bronze Age. Egypt was the dominant power at the time, and these events took place during the Middle Kingdom of the Egyptian dynasties. The Pyramids, and the written word, were already a thousand years old. Sarah's ancestors were desert nomads in Mesopotamia who had no group consciousness. It remained for her and Abraham to give the tribe a sense of being God's chosen people and to weld them into a nation.

When I wrote Sarah's story, I had not yet read Elise Boulding's *The Underside of History*. She suggests that Sarah (or *Sarai*, as she was known then) may have been the leader of the tribe. She indicates that historians dispute whether such tribes were matrilineal. Her study of the period in general makes her feel that they probably were.[1] I have not rewritten the story in the light of her insight. Since I originally thought of Sarah, Rebekah and Rachel as one continuous multi-generational story, I have kept them together in this volume, although Lot's wife belongs between Sarah and Rebekah chronologically.

Lot's wife began to haunt me while I worked on Sarah's story. We were in the process of moving from Friends World College on Long Island to the new Friends Community at North Easton, Massachusetts. Soon after we moved I saw Rosalind Cobb's sculpture of Lot's wife. The face seemed to register horror, helplessness, and compassion; my mind and heart became obsessed with her. As a child in Sunday School I had been told she was a horrible example of disobedience. "Why are we enjoined from looking back?" I asked myself. I was going through the emotional process of leave-taking at the time; we were moving from a house full of memories, a congenial job, a Friends meeting that was a "beloved community," a warm circle of supportive friends, and a dearly-loved campus community. I had to do much looking back and taking leave before I could turn to the new life, and I felt deeply for

---

[1] Elise Boulding, *The Underside of History: A View of Women through Time* (Boulder, Colorado: Westview Press, 1976) p. 236, 273 fn. 9, and elsewhere.

the woman who paused on the hill to take leave of her home, her city.

There is virtually no material on Lot's wife in the Bible. She is mentioned only twice, first in the Old Testament: "But Lot's wife behind him looked back, and she became a pillar of salt" (Gen. 19:26). And Jesus tells us, "Remember Lot's wife" (Luke 17:32). What he said preceding that makes it sound like he subscribes to the horrible-example theory. But he follows it by that enigmatic statement: "Whoever seeks to gain his life will lose it, but whoever loses his life will preserve it" (Luke 17:33). Salt is a powerful preservative.

Remember Lot's wife! Remember all the humble, ordinary human beings, eking out their existence, caring for their families as well as they can, helping their neighbors, struggling with problems too big for them. Then they are caught in cataclysmic forces that ruin their lives: earthquakes, floods, hurricanes, volcanic eruptions, pestilence, economic depression, crop failures, wars, pogroms, lynch mobs. I remember times in my own life when the tears, sometimes unshed and piling up inside, sometimes flowing fountain-like for days and soaking the bed at night, finally stiffened me into a pillar of salt. There are times in every life that simply have to be endured. Remember Lot's wife!

The story of Lot's wife is, then, wholly my imagination. To write it I read various commentaries and what I could find on the city of Haran and the nomads in Canaan. I hope my story may deter Sunday School teachers from trying to keep mischievous students in line by telling them about Lot's wife and the horrible consequences of disobedience.

For Miriam I browsed in Egyptian history and read what I could on the conditions of women in North Africa during the centuries before the Christian era. In writing her story, I took my cue from the statement in which God says: "I sent before you Moses, Aaron, and Miriam" (Mic. 6:4). God called *all three* to lead the Israelites out of bondage. I came to identify very much with Miriam, as one called by God while still a child. I also identified with her when Moses repudiates her calling (Numbers, chapter 12), for I grew up in a denomination that did not ordain women until long after I had decided not to pursue the professional ministry further but to join the Religious

Society of Friends and follow a nonprofessional ministry.

Miriam lived at a time when women in Egypt and other parts of North Africa were well educated and held positions of leadership. I assume Hebrew women did not share this, since the Hebrews were slaves. Moses had the advantage of a palace education and must have towered over his nomadic followers. But I assume he also needed the special gifts of his siblings: Aaron's eloquence and Miriam's gift of prophecy.

I first thought to ignore the puzzling reference to Moses' having married a Cushite woman (Num. 12:1). My sculptor-neighbor Rosalind Cobb is also an Africanist, and persuaded me not to pass over this exciting possibility. She told me of the advanced civilization in East Africa south of Egypt at the time. It was a time of much travel, and on the way to Canaan Moses might well have encountered and been drawn to an African woman with as much education as he had.

In *The Lost Cities of Africa* by Basil Davidson, I read that for nearly a thousand years the Cushite civilization of Napata and Maroe was a major center for exchange of "ways of thought, belief, and manufacture."[1] Elise Boulding also comments on women who ruled as queens and others who fought on horseback under the leadership of a queen in the time of Ramses II.[2]

Then I turned back to that strange story in the New Testament (Acts 8:26-40) where on the road from Jerusalem to Gaza, Philip encounters "an Ethiopian, a eunuch, a minister of the Candace, queen of the Ethiopians, in charge of all her treasure . . ." and converts him. So I let Moses find himself a comely, highly educated black wife on the way to Canaan.

Tamar's story should have come before Miriam's chronologically, for she belongs to a time before the Hebrews went to Egypt, but I wanted to keep her with the other foremothers in the genealogy of Jesus in Matthew.

When I began to read these four stories in the Old Testament, I was impressed that at least three of them were not "good Jewish girls." Tamar and Rahab were Canaanites, Ruth a Moabite, and Bathsheba possibly a Hittite, since her husband

---

[1] Basil Davidson, *The Lost Cities of Africa* (Boston: Little, Brown and Co., 1959) p. 40 ff.
[2] Elise Boulding, *op. cit.,* p. 234.

is always identified as Uriah the Hittite. On the basis of internal evidence, however, I came to think Uriah was a convert to Judaism and Bathsheba a Hebrew. The Canaanites, Moabites, and Hittites were all enemy tribes. My husband suggests that these women "enlarged the gene pool" and kept the house of Abraham from becoming too ingrown. One might add that they bear witness to Paul's assertion:

> There is neither Jew nor Greek, there is neither slave nor free, there is neither male nor female; for you are all one in Christ Jesus. And if you are Christ's then you are Abraham's offspring, heirs according to promise [Gal. 3:28-29].

I also found that not one of these women was moral and upright by Christian standards as we have come to know them. Even gentle Ruth crawled into bed with Boaz to put pressure on him to marry her. Reading these four stories we can say that God sometimes uses people "whose names would not have occurred to us" to further the divine purposes. Placing them in a patriarchal setting, we find them women of courage, determination, and resourcefulness. They took charge of their lives and turned betrayal, defeat, grief, and remorse into something triumphant and good.

Tamar's story in Genesis, chapter 38, is an interruption of the story of Joseph and his brothers. Though we are shocked at the idea of playing the harlot and seducing one's father-in-law, the writer of the story saw Tamar as "righteous," in contrast to Potiphar's wife in the next chapter. To recreate her story, I had to set aside my own twentieth century ideas of right and wrong to feel out her situation. As James Russell Lowell reminds us, "New occasions teach new duties. Time makes ancient good uncouth."

Rahab's story concerns taking Canaan after the Exodus and follows Miriam's chronologically. There is a small problem with Matthew's genealogy. He puts Rahab and Salmon only four generations back from David, making Rahab David's great-great-grandmother. The battle of Jericho took place about 1200 B.C. and David became king two hundred years later in 1002. It seems likely there were more than four generations in two hundred years.

Were there two Rahabs? If so, we know nothing of the second one. Why then would Matthew have included her in his list? I think we can assume he meant the Rabab of Jericho, for she is held in great esteem. In the eleventh chapter of Hebrews, that great chapter on faith, only two women are mentioned among many men as examples of faith: Sarah and Rahab. The Epistle of James, which follows Hebrews, cites her as an example of justification by works. Who else has been given as an example of both faith and works? She may have been a harlot, but she is highly regarded.

Ruth's story has a purpose. When the Hebrews returned from exile in Babylon, Ezra, Nehemiah and others sought to weld Israel into a nation again and felt the men must give up their non-Jewish wives acquired during the exile. At that time an unknown writer wrote a charming story to remind people that David, their much-loved king when their fortunes were at their highest, had Moabite blood. Ruth was his great-grandmother. The writer constantly calls her "Ruth the Moabite" to make the point and ends the story with a short genealogy of David. The story took place some five or six hundred years before the writing, when Israel was not yet a kingdom. It begins "In the days when the judges ruled . . ." — almost like "Once upon a time . . ."

Bathsheba's story was the most difficult one for me. The Bible does not make clear what we are to think of her. Is she innocent victim or willing accomplice? Her son Solomon wrote the book of Proverbs. Is she the loose woman whose lips "drip honey and whose tongue is smoother than oil," of its fifth chapter? Or, is she the virtuous woman whose "price is above rubies" of the last chapter?

I have learned that one should never judge another person without walking in her shoes. As I tried to walk in Bathsheba's sandals and they came to fit my feet more comfortably, I found myself more and more on her side, and in the end, I was wholly partisan.

Friends have always believed in "continuing revelation." I know that new light and truth have come to me from reading the Bible from the women's point of view.

# DAUGHTERS OF ZION

# Sarah

Background: Genesis 11-23

*By faith Sarah herself received power to conceive,
even when she was past the age, since she considered
him faithful who had promised. Therefore from one
man, and him as good as dead, were born descendants
as many as the stars of heaven and as the innumerable
grains of sand by the seashore* [Heb. 11:11-12].

*Sarah!* There! I've written my name and let it stand by itself! All my life I've had to take my identity from someone else. First I was Sarah-daughter-of-Terah. Then I was Sarah-wife-of-Abraham. And in old age I have been Sarah-mother-of-Isaac. But I'm really Sarah, just Sarah. I'm a human being with feelings and brains and intuition. Already the legends about Abraham are growing, but when the historians come to write his story, they are going to have to include me too. I was there. I had a hand in things.

I am old now, more than 125 years old. Most of the time now I sit in my tent and remember, but sometimes I like to look ahead. God promised that our descendants would be more numerous than the stars. I know that a good half of them will be women like me — my granddaughters, and great-granddaughters, generation after generation, as long as the earth endures. Will they think of me sometimes, feeling their way back into my feelings, sharing my remorse for some things I did, and my joy in others? The same tides of longing will flow through their lives as have flowed through mine.

I live in a time when women do not have many rights. Husbands acquire wives like they buy sheep and cattle. Heaven help the woman whose husband is cruel, for men have absolute authority over their wives and children and slaves. Men think the main purpose of women is to produce sons. Many years went by and I had no children. I was called "barren." If Abraham had not loved me, life would indeed have been barren. But still, all those years I was aware of unused energy, unused ability. I longed to do great things, to be used by God for some noble purpose, as Abraham was. Men think God speaks only to them. Finally God spoke to me and I knew beyond doubt that my life was important too. Why did God give us ability if we are not to use it?

I was born in Ur in the southern part of Babylonia. Terah, my father, was head of our large extended family. He had many flocks of sheep and several wives. My mother was one of the younger ones, and she died when I was very young. I do not remember her. I always felt I had to live for both of us. My father was very tender with his motherless little daughter, so I grew up with a sense of his protection and love and had more self-confidence than many women in our tribe. He called me Sarai, a strange name, for it means "mockery." Later God told my husband that my name was really Sarah, which means Princess. I liked that name! I felt like a princess much of my life.

The people of Ur were pagans, with much looser moral standards than we had. We kept pretty much to ourselves because Terah did not want us to be corrupted, nor did he want us to marry outside our own group. When his eldest son was ready to be married, Terah chose me for his wife. Abram and I had different mothers, so it was thought to be all right. Abram means "noble father," so right from the beginning it was expected that he would carry on the tribe. Later God changed his name to Abraham which means "father of multitudes." It seemed like a strange name at the time, for we had no children at all.

I felt very lucky to be Abraham's bride. I'd been in love with him since I was a little girl. He was ten years older than I, and he was tall and good-looking with an air of assurance. He was also righteous and just, but most important, he loved me. All our lives it was fun to share the common memories of brother and sister, but we were also lovers.

Abraham had two brothers. Nahor, the next oldest, married Milcah. Haran, the third, died young, leaving a little boy named Lot who became Abraham's and my responsibility. This helped to make up for my not having any sons of my own.

Conditions in Ur finally became impossible. A wild desert tribe called the Amorites poured into our area, looking for some means of livelihood. They stole our animals and harrassed us. Terah finally decided we must move. He had heard that Canaan was fertile and uncrowded. We made sturdy tents to carry with us, packed up all our belongings, gathered the herds together, and set forth. We followed the Euphrates River valley in a northwesterly direction. The animals had to keep grazing, and continually they had to be herded so they would not stray, so travel was slow. We went on month after month, journeying about 550 miles altogether.

It was especially hard for the women. Most of us had to walk. We had to prepare meals over hastily built fires out of what we could find along the way. Children had to be cared for and carried when they were small. Babies were born. Women were left behind to sweat out their labor and then they had to hurry to catch up before they were really ready to travel. People died and were buried and left behind, and we knew we would never visit their graves again.

We noticed that Terah was getting slower, as time went on, and could no longer go as far in a day. Finally he became ill, and could go no further. We were at a fertile place, so we made a more permanent camp there. We were on the outskirts of the great Amorite city of Haran. It was good to stop traveling. We women hoped we'd never move on. Terah died, and we buried him there. Abraham now became head of the tribe. He built an altar to our God, and we knew that meant he intended to stay. Our God is Yahweh, the God of Justice and Righteousness, the one true God. We do not have idols like the pagan tribes.

From childhood on Abraham had a strong sense of God's presence. God often spoke to him, and if Yahweh told Abraham to do something, there was no stopping him. If Yahweh promised something, Abraham believed it, despite all the evidence against it. He had tremendous faith. I often had doubts about Abraham's messages from God, for it usually meant doing something difficult or unpleasant, sometimes things that seemed utter folly.

One day Abraham called us all together and told us we were to leave our comfortable home and set out for a new land God had promised to us and our descendants. His brother Nahor grumbled and said God hadn't told *him* to move on, so he would stay. Our nephew Lot decided to come along, with his family and flocks. And so by faith — Abraham's faith, that is — we set out. We left home, not knowing where we were to go. We became tent dwellers again.

It was hard to share Abraham's vision, for the land around us did not seem like a "promised land." Food was scarce, and became scarcer as we went on. Finally even Abraham admitted there was a famine, and we joined other desert people headed for Egypt and the fertile Nile valley, where there was said to be food.

Now my Abraham had one fault — jealousy. I was a pretty little girl and said to be quite beautiful when I grew up. I was still attractive when I got to be quite old, for men still turned to look at me wherever we went. Beauty can be a curse. Abraham's jealousy made him do foolish things, and I often wished I were less attractive. He always wanted to show me off and then flew into a rage if people stared at me.

When we reached the border of Egypt, Abraham did a stupid thing, which didn't show much faith in Yahweh, or in me either. He told people I was his sister, instead of his wife. He was afraid someone might kill him in order to marry me. Now it did happen that some men of the court saw us and told Pharaoh about me. Before I knew what was happening, I was taken to the palace. Abraham told me to stick to the story about being his sister. Pharaoh gave him sheep and oxen, asses and camels, slaves and goods — so much that Abraham became wealthy overnight. He didn't seem to care what happened to his wife. I was in danger of landing in Pharaoh's harem. I prayed and Yahweh answered my prayer in a strange way. Instead of punishing Abraham, he sent plagues on the court. Pharaoh finally guessed the reason. He sent for Abraham and asked why he hadn't said I was his wife. Abraham had no good answer. We were escorted to the border and told to leave Egypt.

I was really angry and outraged. Abraham felt proud to have tricked Pharaoh out of all those gifts and would not return them. I complained bitterly. To try to appease me, he gave me one of the slaves he had been given. It was nice to have a slave of my own, but it didn't make up for all I'd been through. In time I got over the unhappy experience, but I'm sorry to say it was not the only time it happened.

We wandered again in the desert. After many weeks we saw a landmark in the distance — an oasis with a grove of trees. It had been a holy place for generations and was called The Oaks of Mamre. We made camp there. God appeared to Abraham and told him to look around, as far as he could see in all directions. This was the land promised to us. Abraham built an altar there and we settled down.

The slave girl Abraham gave me when we left Egypt was called Hagar. She served me faithfully and I came to love and trust her. It was good to have another woman in whom to confide. By this time I was definitely past the child-bearing age, and had had no children. According to our custom, I gave Abraham my slave to see if she might have a son whom I could adopt. No one will know how much it hurt me to do this. I cried in my tent night after night, while my husband slept with her and made love to her.

Hagar became pregnant almost at once, and then she abruptly changed toward me. Her new status as Abraham's concubine went to her head. She turned on me and mocked me for having no children. One day I reached the breaking point and struck her blindly, in fury. She ran away heedlessly, right out into the desert, without water. She was soon lost and thirsty. Yahweh told her to look around, and she found a spring near by. She came back and things were better for a while, but we were never close again.

When her son was born, he was named Ishmael, which means "God has heard my prayer." Abraham was overjoyed and lavished much love on him. He was a strange boy. From the time he could walk, he wandered off alone. When he grew to be a young man he was sullen. He seemed more at home in the desert than he did with the tribe. He seemed to feel everyone was against him, and he in turn was against everyone. It was hard to understand him, for he did not fit into our life.

Years went by, for the most part uneventful. The desert has its special ways, its etiquette. The stranger is always the guest. You give travelers food and water, even if supplies are scarce and the family does without. You do this for strangers, whoever they may be. Strangers are always welcome. They bring news, and things to trade. They break the monotony of life and give a sense of the human community beyond the tribe. Sometimes they turn out to be messengers of God — angels in disguise.

So it happened one day that Abraham was resting in the doorway of his tent, when he looked up and saw three travelers coming across the sand in the distance. He put his head inside my tent and told me to make some bread and get food ready. He gave instructions for an animal to be killed and roasted, and water to be drawn. He went out to meet the travelers and urged them to stop awhile. Right away we knew these were no ordinary guests. They were messengers from God and told Abraham that within a year I would give birth to a son. I could not help but hear what was said as I worked in the tent. I was ninety years old now, and Abraham was a hundred years old. Here was this same old joke about my having children. I thought Abraham's God certainly did not know much about women! I laughed bitterly, and could not stop laughing. I became hysterical.

Suddenly the tent flap was flung aside. I found myself looking into the face of a stranger, only I couldn't see the face. I fell to my knees and covered my head. For the first time in my life I knew I was in the presence of God. The awareness of God's existence blotted out everything else and filled the universe, encompassing everything. I understood why we sometimes call our God the *Great I Am.*

I heard God speak my name: Sarah! Whether God spoke out loud or in my head, I'm not sure, but I know Yahweh spoke to me. I was told I would have my longed-for son, if I had faith that it was possible. And I knew, beyond doubt, that nothing is impossible to God if we have faith. It is never too late to be a channel for God's life and love.

I had always been told that God speaks only to men, but now I knew that God speaks to women too. From now on I would be Abraham's partner, not just his follower. From now on I too believed in the dream that had kept him traveling by faith those long years in the desert — the dream of the City of God, blossoming like the rose, in the desert.

I got up from my knees. I was alone. The years seemed to fall from me. My body seemed to grow straighter and lighter. The days that followed were full of grace, amazing grace. My work came easy. "Now faith is the substance of things hoped for, the evidence of things not seen" (Heb. 11:1 KJ). Before long my body confirmed my heart's faith. I knew I would indeed have a child. Soon everyone else could see it also.

Our son was born within a year, and we named him Isaac, which means "God laughed." The name had a double meaning. I had laughed at God, and now God was laughing at my lack of faith. But more important, laughter is a sign of joy, and

Abraham and I both felt God shared our happiness. Our son was as beautiful as his father had been as a boy, and looked much like him.

Only one thing spoiled my joy. Hagar still acted as though she had the number one son. We held a great feast when Isaac was weaned, and there was Ishmael in the middle of things, bidding for attention. I finally persuaded Abraham that we should give Hagar her freedom and send her and Ishmael back to Egypt. They had to go. When a caravan bound for Egypt passed, we sent them off with provisions and water. Once again Hagar stubbornly wandered off on her own, and Ishmael nearly died of thirst. Again Yahweh showed her a spring near by. They settled down at Paran. We kept in touch with them.

Ishmael grew up to be a mighty hunter, skilled with the bow. He understood the birds and animals in a way that he never understood people. He scorned civilization and its ways. There was always something untamed about him. Hagar finally found him a wife in Egypt, and he became head of a large family.

It was right for them to go. Even Abraham, when he asked God about it, received assurance I was right. Isaac clearly was the one to inherit Abraham's vast property and position of leadership. Ishmael could never have carried such responsibility. (Sometimes I remember my early love for Hagar and ask myself how I could have kept things from going wrong. It was so beautiful when we were close and could talk about things together. I really needed her, and I think she needed me. I wish we might have lived out our lives in peace together, but neither of us had the maturity or generosity or faith to make it work.)

Our Isaac grew and developed into a wonderful boy and everyone loved him. Through him something of us — of Abraham and Sarah — will live forever. So in my old age there came a time of great serenity and quiet joy.

One day, however, I woke later than usual and was slow to get moving. I was now too old to push myself. It seemed strange that Isaac had not come in and waked me. He was always wanting to show me something or tell me of his boyish activities. I finally asked one of the servants if she had seen him, and she said Abraham had gone off with him very early, taking two of his men and a load of firewood. He said they would be gone several days. Why hadn't he told me he was planning a trip? It was not like him to sneak off with Isaac without telling me. I told myself he was getting old and forgetful, but fear clutched at my heart. The days dragged by and I could not sleep.

Finally they returned. Something had obviously happened to Isaac. He came running into my tent, flung himself into my arms and sobbed uncontrollably. It was some time before I could piece the story together. His father had told him they were going to a distant altar to make a sacrifice to Yahweh, and he cautioned him not to tell me. He was very proud to be included. Isaac was puzzled that they took wood, but no animals, for he had seen his father go off other times with rams or goats to sacrifice. He asked his father about it, and Abraham told him God would provide the sacrifice. When they arrived at the place, with no warning, Abraham seized Isaac, bound him, laid him on the altar and raised the knife to kill him. Only at the last moment had Yahweh stopped him. A ram was found in the thicket and sacrificed instead.

I confronted Abraham and demanded an explanation. He said that God was testing his faith. If God told him to sacrifice his son, then he must do it. Isaac was a gift from God, and if God wanted him back, that was the way it had to be.

I told him that if God had really wanted Isaac back, some other way would have been found than having his own father kill him. Of course Isaac was a gift from God, but Yahweh is the God of life, not death. I believed God wanted us to bring up our son so that he would walk with God all his days and belong to God all his life. (Women know, in a way that men do not, how long it takes to bring a human life into being. They cooperate with God in giving birth to a new human soul, and in their pain and labor they are close to God. They know too how many hazards there are as children grow. Life is precious. It is to be cherished and nurtured, never taken for granted, never cheapened with unnecessary violence.)

Abraham humbly replied that he knew that now. Yahweh had spoken to him there at the altar and told him that what was required was not human sacrifice, but "to do justly, to love mercy, and to walk humbly with God" (Micah 6:8).

Abraham was concerned about Isaac and tried to be very tender with him. However, I'm not sure Isaac ever got over the memory of the experience. For a long time his sleep was troubled, and during the day he kept close to me. I comforted him and assured him his father would never do such a thing again. Isaac still clings to me, although he is a grown man now. I worry what will happen to him when I die, for I cannot live much longer. I have made Abraham promise to find a wife for him from among our own people back at Haran. I think of my unknown daughter-in-law and wish I might see her and know her in the flesh. I have faith that she will comfort Isaac and give him back his self-confidence.

I do not want people to think that Abraham and I have always had our differences. The jealousy of his early years and the times we have disagreed seem really trifles compared to the long years we have lived together and loved one another. And the last thirty-five years have been especially happy, since Yahweh spoke to me and faith was born in me. We have shared that faith and the knowledge of God's goodness and steadfast love for us. How different our lives would have been if Abraham had not had faith.

By faith Abraham obeyed when God called him to go out to a place which he was to receive as an inheritance; and we went out, not knowing where we were to go. By faith we sojourned in the land of promise, as in a foreign land, living in tents. For we look forward to the city which has foundations, whose builder and maker is God. By faith I myself received power to conceive, even when I was past the age, since I considered God faithful who had promised. Therefore, from one man, and him as good as dead [— well, what can you expect from a man who is a hundred years old? —] will be born descendants as many as the stars of heaven and as the innumerable grains of sand by the seashore (see Hebrews 11:8-12).

O you who come after me, my daughters of all the generations, pray for faith. Pray that the way may open for you to be used by God, according to your gifts. Have faith that God can use you, whatever your age, whatever your circumstances. You are never too old to be used by God. Likewise you are never too young. No one is beyond hope.

And all of you, my sons and my daughters in ages to come, have faith in the City of God. Believe in the Promised Land where no one will hurt or destroy, where all will live together in peace and mutual support. And go right forward to claim it.

# Rebekah

Background: Genesis 22-27

*And they called Rebekah, and said to her, "Will you go with this man?" She said, "I will go...."*
*And they blessed Rebekah, and said to her, "Our sister, be the mother of thousands of ten thousounds..."* [Gen. 24:58, 60].

*Rebekah!* I've written *my* name and let it stand alone, just like Sarah did! But on second thought, I'm not sure I want it to stand alone. Instead, I think I'll write: Rebekah, daughter-in-law of Sarah! How I wish she'd still been alive when I came to Canaan to marry Isaac! How I wish I could have known her and talked to her and had her to turn to for advice. I have needed her wisdom, her experience, her faith. It's lonely, being a woman. I've had no other woman I could talk to about important things. Men, no matter how much you love them, don't ever see things quite the same way.

I never did acquire Sarah's hard-won faith. I think faith is a gift from God, an act of grace. And God never gave it to me. God gave me *hope* instead. Hope means that anything is possible, even when it's not probable. With hope, life is a great adventure, and "if life is not a great adventure, it's nothing."[1] And "to refuse the adventure life sends,"[2] is to refuse everything.

I have a strange name. Rebekah is the Hebrew word for Noose. I am told I was born with the cord around my neck and nearly died in the process of birth. Even then I was fighting for a chance, eager to be alive. Now, at the end of my life, I hope I have not been a noose strangling those I love. It is true: I deceived my husband and I cheated one of my sons out of his most precious possession.

I need to set my story down to help me understand why I had to do those things. Also, like Sarah, I look ahead to the

---

[1] I borrowed this phrase from Helen Keller. —ew
[2] And this one I've borrowed from C.S. Lewis, *The Chronicles of Narnia,* Book 1, "The Lion, the Witch and the Wardrobe." —ew

promised generations of our children. I want my grand-daughters, and great-granddaughters, generation after generation, to know why I felt I had to do those things, to give some account of the hope that is in me, for without hope my life doesn't make sense.

Some day, surely, Jacob will come home again. He must have a wife and children by now. I long to see my unknown daughter-in-law, just as Sarah longed to see me. But Jacob's been gone twenty long years now, and I will probably die before he brings his family home, just as Sarah died before I came. Realistically I know I have not much longer to live. However, I still keep hoping each day to see Jacob's caravan coming across the desert.

I was born in Haran. I am the granddaughter of Nahor, Abraham's younger brother, who stayed behind when Abraham and Sarah and Lot set out to look for the Promised Land. My father was Bethuel. He and Isaac were first cousins. Isaac was born so late in his parents' life that a whole generation was skipped.

Life in Haran was settled and quite comfortable and my girlhood was happy. I had an older brother, Laban, who liked to tease me. He was really devoted to me, and I learned to take his teasing and shrug it off. He was a great practical joker. I had a great deal of freedom for a girl in those days. However, life often seemed dull, and I found it too calm and peaceful. I longed for some great adventure to come my way. I longed to do important things in the world. I daydreamed a good deal and hoped something exciting would happen.

And so it did. It was my task to go to the town well every day for water, and I loved that time of day. Everyone gathered at the well. I could see my friends there and sometimes I could pick up news to take back to the family, for travelers stopped there. One day I took my water jar on my shoulder as usual. When I came within sight of the well, I saw there were strangers there — one man who looked important and several attendants. They had a whole string of camels. They must have been traveling a long time, for their clothes and hair were dusty. Even the camels' tongues were hanging out, showing they had used up all their water.

I filled my water jar, wondering if I should offer some to the strangers. I hoped the man who seemed to be in charge would say something to me, for it was not proper for me to speak first. Sure enough, he did. He asked if I would give him and his men a drink, so I let down the water jar from my shoulder and tipped it so that he could drink, and I gave each of the men in turn a chance to drink. I felt sorry for the camels, so I said, "I will draw water for your camels too."

Then the most amazing thing happened. After the camels had drunk their fill, the man produced a gold nose ring and two beautiful gold bracelets, intricately worked. He held them out to me, and when I held back, he insisted on putting the bracelets on my arms. I loved the feel of them. The man asked whose daughter I was, and if there might be room for him and his party to lodge with us for the night. We were always hospitable to strangers, of course, so I told him that we did have room, and that I was the daughter of Bethuel, who was the son of Nahor and Milcah. And this produced an extraordinary reaction. The man fell to his knees and began to pray out loud. To this day I remember his words: "Blessed be the Lord, the God of my master Abraham, who has not forsaken his steadfast love and his faithfulness toward my master. As for me, the Lord has led me in the way to the house of my master's kinsmen" (Gen. 24:27).

When I grasped that this man was the servant of Uncle Abraham, I dashed back to alert the family to get ready for company. My brother Laban looked at the bracelets on my arms and whistled. He could see they were expensive and he always wanted to cultivate people with money. He ran back to the well to find the man and fell all over himself trying to be helpful. He found a pen for the camels and brought water for the men to wash their feet. By this time food was ready, but the man was much too excited to eat. He said he had to tell us his message first. He told us his name was Eliezer, trusted servant of Abraham.

Then we learned that Uncle Abraham and Aunt Sarah had had a wonderful child in their old age named Isaac, and that Sarah had made Abraham promise before she died that he would send back to find a wife for Isaac from among their own people at Haran. This was the task Eliezer had undertaken. He said that when he finally reached our well in Haran, he prayed that if the first young woman who came to the well gave him a drink and then offered to water the camels, this would be a sign from God that she was the right one. Amazingly enough, I had said all the right things.

My father and Laban said at once, "This is the Lord's doing." Then Eliezer gave me many gifts, and there were presents for my mother and father and brother too. Finally we got around to eating the food that had been prepared, and long before we finished eating the sun had gone down and it was time to sleep.

Well, I didn't sleep much that night. My head was in a whirl. I'd hoped for an adventure, and now it had come. But when I realized that I would probably never see my family and my home again, I was sad and just a little afraid to be going off to marry someone I had never seen. I prayed a long time. The sense that this was God's will for me came over me, and I finally was able to settle down and sleep. I hoped I would love Isaac. More than that I hoped he would love me and be good to me.

Abraham's servant was up at the first light and was all for starting right back. My mother asked if he couldn't stay ten days at least, so there would be time to make some preparation for a wedding and gather my things together. We all needed a little time to get used to the idea. But Eliezer was impatient. He was afraid Abraham might die while he was gone on this long journey, and he could hardly wait to share his news with his master.

My family did an unusual thing. They called me and asked if I really wanted to go off with this man. I had not realized I had a choice, and for a moment I did not know what to say. Then a strong sense of its being God's will came over me, and I answered confidently, "I will go." I would not turn back from the adventure that had come to me.

We ate quickly and I gathered my things together. It helped to ease the parting that Deborah, my nurse from childhood, would be coming too. (She has lived to a great age and has always been a great help to me, though by now she is quite deaf and somewhat childish. I think she will probably outlive me.)

Finally the moment came to say good-bye to my family. They all gathered around and each one in turn kissed me and gave me a blessing. Laban said, "Our sister, be the mother of thousands of ten thousands . . ." (Gen. 24:60). I often remember his words and think of the generations of my children for all the years to come, just as Sarah did. My father and Laban helped Deborah and me climb up on the camels and we settled ourselves as comfortably as we could for the long journey to Canaan.

We plodded along, day after day. Sometimes the tears ran down my face as I was carried farther and farther from all that I knew and loved. Then Deborah would reach out to comfort me, and hope would rise in me again, and I would look forward eagerly to whatever was to come. But it is true: I never did see my family again.

After many weeks we approached the Negev region where Isaac and the tribe were sojourning. One afternoon I saw a man in the distance, walking in the fields.

He seemed to be meditating or praying as he walked. It had been days since we had seen anyone, and my heart turned over at sight of this man. I asked Eliezer who this might be. Then he recognized Isaac, and told me this was the man who was to be my husband. By this time Isaac had seen us coming, so I quickly jumped down from my camel and put my veil over my face.

Eliezer told Isaac everything that had happened, and Isaac came and took me by the hand. We were married that very day, and in the evening he led me to one of the tents. He told me that this had been his mother's tent, and now it would be mine. The tears ran down his face as he spoke of her. He was still grieving for her. My heart went out to him. I took him in my arms and comforted him, and I loved him for his gentleness, his sensitivity, and the goodness which shone in his face. (He had needed someone to talk to, as he had confided in his mother, and it is the joy of my life that in some measure I could fill that place in his life. He has told me so much about Sarah that I know her well. Sometimes she seems more alive to me than the people around me.)

Abraham, too, was deeply glad that I had come, and we too loved one another from the beginning. He was very old now, and very frail. He had been keeping himself alive until Eliezer should return with a wife for Isaac.

Sometimes Isaac talked to me about his half-brother, Ishmael. He was troubled that he and his mother had been sent away. I urged Isaac to send Eliezer now to see if Ishmael could be found, in the hope that he would come before Abraham died. We had no assurance he could be found, or that he would want to come, but we both hoped he might. Ishmael did come, arriving before Abraham died, and they did have a little time to be together. Ishmael helped Isaac bury him in the tomb beside Sarah, and the two brothers threw their arms around each other and wept together for their father. They parted in peace.

The years went by. Sometimes there were good harvests, sometimes famine. At times there were disputes with other tribes about wells; for water, of course, was scarce, and very necessary for both people and animals. Isaac had a knack of finding water. He was always gentle and unaggressive. He would willingly give up a well he had dug, if a dispute arose, for he had faith that Yahweh would always help him find more water. Finally he found a great well, and here he made a covenant to live at peace with Abimelech, leader of a tribe that had been disputing with us. They called the place Beer-sheba, which means "well of the oath." Abimelech and the other chieftains recognized that Isaac was a just man and that our God was with us and would protect us.

I understood so well how Sarah felt when she was called "barren," for, like her, I had no children for a long time. Isaac never lost faith that we would eventually have children, and I hoped, but did not have much faith. Isaac prayed confidently, year after year, and eventually his prayers were answered. But twenty years had gone by since our marriage and I was no longer young. It was a most difficult pregnancy. Sometimes I felt I might not live through it. Life seemed hardly worth living.

Isaac suggested I make a pilgrimage to a holy place and ask Yahweh about it. I did. Yahweh told me that I would have twins, and they were already at war within me, as they would be in life. Yahweh told me further that the older one should serve the younger one, and the line of blessing pass through the one born second. I knew this would mean trouble, for it is a sacred thing that the older son is the heir. At the time I was sure I heard God rightly, but sometimes in the years that followed I wondered if I got the message entirely straight.

Finally my time came and the twins were born. The first was hairy and red, and we named him Esau, which is a pun on the word for red. His brother came out almost simultaneously, hanging on to his heel, so we named him Jacob, which is a pun on the word heel. But it also means "May God protect," which seemed a good name, in view of the predictions about the relationship of the two brothers. This smaller second son was going to need God's protection.

It is strange how early in life the patterns are set. From early childhood, Esau loved the out-of-doors, and by the time he was half grown it was obvious that he was at home with wild things and understood their ways. He became a fine hunter and we all enjoyed the savory dishes he made from the game he brought home. But if *I* told him to do something, he never seemed to hear me. He went his own way without paying attention. If I remonstrated, he ran off, or talked back rudely. I did my best to bring him up to be responsible, but he just would not take responsibility. Isaac had more patience. He remembered Ishmael and was sympathetic to this son who in some ways resembled him. A bond grew between Isaac and Esau, and I quit trying to bring up Esau to be a civilized human being.

Jacob was just the opposite. From the time he was a small boy he always wanted to please me. "Let me do it, mother," he would say. He took to the life of the herdsman, and always carried more than his share of the work. He saw things that needed doing and did them. From the beginning he was clever and people liked him. Surely the message I had received was right. Jacob was the one who could take over the tribe after his father died. But how to bring it about? I talked to Isaac about it, but he always wanted to avoid conflict. "It will work itself out," he said, "have faith." I couldn't see any justification for faith, but I did keep hoping.

So the boys grew up, their ways diverging more and more. One day Esau had been out hunting and had not had his usual luck. He came home very late, tired and not feeling well. He was ravenous, not having eaten all day. Jacob was making lentil soup and Esau asked for a bowl. Jacob is shrewd, like my brother Laban, and half-joking, half in earnest, he offered him a bowl of soup in return for Esau's birthright. So, thoughtlessly, carelessly, the deal was made. When Jacob told me about it, I was appalled. Did Esau really value his inheritance so little that he would exchange it for a bowl of soup? "For you know that afterward, when he desired to inherit the blessing, he was rejected, for he found no chance to repent, though he sought it with tears" (Hebrews 12:17).

I did not dare tell Isaac. He loved Esau so much and had such faith he would turn out all right. I cautioned Jacob not to tell anyone. As for Esau, he seemed to forget the whole matter. But from then on, I knew I had to be alert for the opportunity to deceive Isaac into giving the inheritance to Jacob.

Poor Isaac! I have loved him so much. He has been such a good and gentle person. But he has never had his father's drive. He wanted to live at peace with everyone. He wanted to be left alone to enjoy his family, to meditate, to walk humbly with God. What would become of us all after he dies, if heedless, careless Esau were at the head of the tribe? Someone had to see to it that Jacob had the inheritance. I had to be the one. There was no one else to do it.

Isaac's eyesight failed him and he grew old and frail. Several times we thought he would not survive an illness. I still cared for him and comforted him, and now I had to be his eyes as well. When I realized he was going blind, I saw that this would make it easier to get him to bless Jacob.

Then one day the chance came. Isaac was sick again and I heard him tell Esau to take his bow, bring back some game, and make the kind of savory stew he loved. Then, he said, he would give Esau his blessing, for he thought he had not much longer to live. So Esau went off, and I knew he would be gone for some time.

I sent for Jacob and told him to get two kids from our herd, so that I could make some stew and season it the way Esau always did. I knew also that we had to give Jacob some of Esau's characteristics or we would never fool Isaac. I took some goatskin and fitted it to Jacob's arms and hands so he would feel hairy, like Esau. I went into Esau's tent and got out his best robe. I sniffed it, and sure enough, it smelled like him. When the stew was ready, my part was done. It was now up to Jacob to carry through the deception. I could only hope and pray that we were doing God's will.

Jacob rose to the occasion and played his part very convincingly. When Isaac asked how he had caught game so soon, Jacob calmly said, "The Lord your God granted me success." He let Isaac feel his hairy arms and hands and sniff for quite a while. Finally Isaac said, "The voice is the voice of

Jacob, but the hands are the hands of Esau," and I knew my plan had worked. Isaac gave him the blessing. And it could not be retracted. (Once the word has been spoken and goes forth, for blessing or for cursing, it can never be taken back.)

Jacob was hardly out of his father's room when we heard Esau come into the courtyard. Jacob kept out of sight and Esau set about making the stew. Finally it was ready and he went expectantly with it to his father. How great was Isaac's consternation when he realized he had been deceived! And how great was Esau's desolation when he realized he had been cheated. Pathetically he asked his father if there was no blessing left for him. Isaac, always prophetic, could only give him a realistic prediction, more curse than blessing:

> Behold, away from the fatness of the earth shall your dwelling be, and away from the dew of heaven on high; By your sword shall you live, and you shall serve your brother . . . (Gen. 27:39-40).

And then he added:

> But when you break loose, you shall break his yoke from your neck.

Now we had to deal with Esau's anger, which was blind and murderous. I feared Jacob would be killed, so I sent him away. But first he went to his father, for he did not want to part from him without making peace. Isaac blessed him again, and told him to go to my brother Laban, and stay there a while, and choose a wife. He did not want him to marry one of the Canaanite women.

I have thought long and hard about Esau. Was I an unnatural mother to turn so against my own son? I have tried to understand Esau. He has scorned civilization; the wild world has been his natural home. He has understood the language of the birds and animals. From his instinctive knowledge of them has come his skill as a hunter. But he has always apologized to the creatures he kills. He has respected them, and loved them. He has not understood the ways of human beings, and has thought the wild creatures are superior to people because they live in harmony with the earth. They are not devious or cruel. They do not kill their own kind. They can be trusted. He has refused to accept responsibility among people, because he has not wanted it. To put it bluntly, Esau has refused to be tamed.

I fear that everyone's hand will be against him, and that as people become more and more civilized and push back the wild places of the earth, he will be hounded out of existence. Sometimes in dreams I see tribes of people like my Esau, killed off by civilized people like us, in the name of progress. I see in my dreams little people called Bushmen, farther south in Africa; I see aborigines in remote islands of the sea, and red people, the color of my Esau, in a new world beyond the great sea. All of them — pushed off their land, hunted down and killed like animals, with no room for them and their way of life. My heart is sick with fear for all the Esaus of the world.

Why cannot there be room for both the Jacobs and the Esaus? If we become too civilized and destroy all the wildness, we will lose something that we need for survival. Are we not destroying part of ourselves? Was God trying to tell me that both sons and their ways are important by the fact that they are twins? And in letting Esau be born first, was God trying to underscore his importance in the world?

I have made my peace with Esau. I went to him and took full responsibility for all that had happened. I told him what had been revealed to me before his birth. He agreed that Jacob was much more suited to take responsibility than he, and he added that in giving up his birthright, he recognized that he had gained freedom to live his own life in his own way. He forgave me fully, freely, and assured me that when Jacob returns from Haran he will welcome and forgive him and will always try to live at peace with him.

Isaac still clings to life, old, and blind, and feeble. He has faith that Jacob will return any day now. All of us long for the day. I fear he will not come soon enough for me to hold him close again and welcome the family he must have by now. But still I hope, for without hope I could not go on. I try to hold things together, so there will be something for Jacob to inherit when he comes home.

Hope seems to me to be the most important thing. It keeps you optimistic. It lets you live with a light touch. It keeps you from becoming a nagger or a killjoy. It keeps you uncomplaining and cheerful.

Hope gives you patience to take each day as it comes, and to endure the infirmities, the stiffness, the slowing down of old age.

But most important, hope gives courage to act when the way is dark and the path full of danger. You can act without counting the cost or figuring the odds for success if you have hope. No one has courage without hope.

My children of all the generations to come, will you believe me? Hope is something very important to cultivate in life. No matter how bad things get, no matter how many disappointments and disasters overtake you, no matter how drab and monotonous life may become, you can always go right forward, day after hum-drum day, if you have hope.

# Rachel

Background: Genesis 29-35

*A voice is heard in Ramah, lamentation and bitter weeping. Rachel is weeping for her children; she refuses to be comforted for her children because they are not.*
*Thus says the Lord:*
*Keep your voice from weeping, and your eyes from tears; for your work shall be rewarded, says the Lord, and they shall come back from the land of the enemy. There is hope for your future, says the Lord* [Jer. 31:15-17].

My name is Rachel. I am Rebekah's daughter-in-law, and also her niece, for Laban, my father, was her brother. She died shortly before Jacob brought us back to Canaan. I often think of her and wish I might have known her. And I often think of Sarah, her mother-in-law. Sarah, the woman of hard-won faith . . . Rebekah, the woman of eternal hope . . . I would like to place my name beside theirs, for we are kindred spirits. But what has characterized my life? What wisdom do I have to pass on to my daughters of all the generations to come? Perhaps if I set it all down, the pattern of my life will become clearer.

I was born in Haran, into the tribe of my great-grandfather, Nahor, the younger brother of Abraham the patriarch. My grandfather was Bethuel, and my father was Laban. My parents had two sons, and then many years later, two daughters. Our brothers were grown up and not home much when Leah and I came along, so, much of the time there were just the two of us. I was the younger sister.

Leah's eyes were crossed, and it made her whole face unattractive. She always tried to compensate by being very good, eager to please, diligent in her work, and very agreeable — that is, to everyone but me. Because she didn't see well, she was somewhat clumsy, and a bit slow of speech. I was just the opposite. I was quick. I felt rhythm and music and I loved to dance. Even as a child I knew I was attractive, for men of all ages turned to look at me whenever I was around. (They still do, even now, when I am pregnant and in pain much of the time.)

When we were girls, Leah mostly stayed indoors. She helped with the cooking. She made clothes and carried a large part of the housework. These things always bored me. I wanted to be outdoors, to do things, to run with the wind, to explore the world, to be with people. I found it hard to keep my clothes clean and my hair brushed, and I never wanted to be inside long enough to straighten up things after myself. Our mother was always punishing me, and then Leah would gloat. She was spiteful and mean, and always telling tales on me. I was often punished for things that would have gone unnoticed if Leah hadn't called them to Mother's attention. We hated each other, and I know that our constant petty bickering poisoned the whole family atmosphere.

Finally it was decided to put me in charge of one of the flocks of sheep the family owned. I was overjoyed. I was now out of the house all day and not expected to do housework. I was outdoors all day and Leah was out of my hair. I fondly looked forward to the day I would be old enough to be married, so I could go away and never have to see her again. She probably felt the same way about me. It must have been hard to be homely and to have a sister everyone thought beautiful.

Water is scarce in our part of the world, and one of my tasks every day was to bring the sheep to the well in the late afternoon to be watered. The well was large with an enormous stone over it. We waited until all the shepherds had brought their flocks and all the women assembled with their pitchers, and then the men all heaved the stone off together. After everyone had drawn water and the sheep had drunk their fill, the big stone was dragged back over the well again. I loved this time of day. Everyone gathered at the well and it was fun to be with people. Travelers often stopped there and rested, waiting till the well was open.

One day when I arrived with my sheep, I saw there was a traveler there — just one man, with no camels. He had evidently been asking about our family, for the shepherds who were already there pointed in my direction, and I saw the man turn to stare at me. I lowered my eyes, but not before I saw that he was very attractive, inspite of the dust of travel on his clothes and hair. This was my Jacob, although I did not know him yet. (He's always been impetuous, and something of a show-off, and he is strong.) The shepherds kept telling him that it was the custom to wait until everyone came, but Jacob didn't want to wait. He stepped up to the well confidently and moved the boulder off by himself, quite a feat of strength. Then he insisted on watering my sheep. While the sheep drank he told me he was Rebekah's son. I had heard of Aunt Rebekah all of my life, but I had never seen her. I was eager to be off to tell the family a relative had come, so I asked him to watch the sheep for me. He said he would, and before I could turn to go, he grabbed me and kissed me. I pulled away and dashed back to our house. When my father heard the news, he hurried off to bring his nephew back to our compound, and I finally got all the sheep safely back in the pen.

My head was spinning. Already I knew I was in love with this man and that I would always love him. I had a sense of destiny. Surely God had brought us together. And I knew, with every inch of my woman's being, that my love was returned.

Bit by bit we learned Jacob's story, how he had tricked his brother out of the blessing, with his mother's help, and how he had had to flee for his life. He clearly wanted to stay a while, so he made himself useful. Laban was eager to have him. I wished I might warn Jacob that my father was a shrewd bargainer, so he should be careful in making any kind of deal with him, but the family saw to it that we were not alone very much.

After Jacob had been with us a month, Laban said, "Why should you serve me for nothing? What wages would you like?" And my Jacob said he would like to work seven years in return for marrying me. I was really too young to be married yet, so everyone agreed this would be an ideal arrangement.

Those were beautiful years, and they flew by. I saw Jacob day after day, and the more I saw him the more I loved him. And I knew that he loved me too. Each day brought us nearer to our wedding and our life together. I did not know that life could hold so much happiness.

During the last months I began sewing and getting things ready for our marriage. At last our day arrived, and everything was in readiness. In the evening we would be married and then go to our own tent to be truly together at last. I had my beautiful clothes and my veil all laid out and began to get dressed. I was so happy I could not keep from dancing around the tent.

Suddenly the tent flap was flung open and I was seized from behind. A hand was clapped over my mouth to stifle my screams. I was tied up and blindfolded and carried off some distance from our main compound. I was shoved into a tent. I finally managed to work the bandage off my eyes. I could hear that someone was outside, keeping watch, but no one came near me. I struggled and struggled but could not free myself. After many hours I could see that it was already getting daylight. My whole wedding night was over. Why had my family allowed me to be kidnapped and had not searched until they found me? Why hadn't Jacob combed the countryside and come and rescued me? I felt utterly abandoned and betrayed.

I was kept under guard a whole week and only then returned home. Then I learned it was my own father who had so ill-used me. He said he had despaired of ever marrying Leah to anyone, so he had decked her out and veiled her, and Jacob had married her and made love to her in the darkness of the tent, all the time thinking he was making love to his Rachel. Now that their marriage week was over, my father said Jacob could marry me too, if he were willing to work another seven years.

It was not only that I missed my wedding night with my beloved. Now I was yoked with the hateful Leah for the rest of my life, destined to be competing with her for the attentions of our mutual husband. How could my happiness so quickly turn to ashes, and at the hands of my own father? I vowed I would get revenge some day.

It did not help that Leah had a son nine months after they were married, and I wasn't even pregnant yet. And she had four sons, about as fast as she could have them, and still I had none. I knew, and she knew too, that Jacob loved me and did not love her. She gave her sons names that emphasized her rivalry with me. She called the first one Reuben, which means, See, A Son! And the second one was Simeon, which means Yahweh Has heard, — that is, God had heard she was not loved. The third son was Levi which means United, — that is, surely now Jacob will be united with her. And the fourth son she named Judah, which means Praise God. Their names were a constant reminder to me of my barrenness. I complained bitterly and even my beloved Jacob grew angry with me.

Like Sarah, I gave Jacob my maid, and when she promptly bore a son, I adopted him, and also a second son that she had later. Leah, not to be outdone, gave Jacob her maid, and she had two sons. And still I had none of my own. Then Leah had two more sons, and a daughter, called Dinah. Now Jacob had ten sons and one daughter, and not one of them had been borne to me.

I prayed. I made sacrifices. I fasted. Finally God answered my prayers. (Now why is it that Leah and our two maids could have children easily, almost painlessly, but with me it was a different story?) It was a difficult pregnancy the whole way, and a long and painful delivery. But my small son was worth waiting for. My Joseph has been my pride and joy. He has always looked more like Jacob than the others, and has had his charm and grace. I have loved to make clothes to show off how beautiful he is. I would gather different plants to dye the wool in various colors, and I have made him an especially beautiful coat which is like a rainbow, it has so many colors.

(Already Joseph shows qualities of leadership. I know he will do great deeds and bring fame to our family. But I worry too. His older brothers are jealous of him. His mind is much quicker than theirs, and like Jacob, he likes to show off his knowledge. He has not yet learned to be tactful. I'm afraid he may be hurt, for I sometimes hear the older boys grumble about him.)

Jacob served out his second seven years, and my father's affairs prospered because of him. Now that Joseph was born, Jacob wanted to return to his own country to see his parents again. He approached Laban about leaving, but my father did not want to let him go. Jacob made a deal that he would work six more years, and instead of being paid in money, he would take all the speckled and spotted sheep and goats. This seemed like a good deal to Laban, and he agreed. He separated the speckled and spotted ones out of his flocks and gave them to Jacob.

My father did not know that my clever Jacob had learned a great deal about animal breeding. Over those six years Jacob was able by selective breeding to produce a large number of speckled and spotted animals, and moreover, to breed those traits into the strong animals. Gradually the weaker animals were all in Laban's flocks, and the stronger ones in Jacob's. Jacob felt completely justified. He was getting even with Laban for his trickery.

Finally Laban and my brothers realized what was happening. My father became very angry and Jacob saw it was time to leave. He asked Leah and me if we were willing to go, and both of us were eager to leave. We waited until Laban was gone for several days at the sheep shearing. Then Jacob gathered all his flocks and herds and family and we all set off. We had gone three days' journey before Laban realized what had happened. He came riding after us post haste, and in a week caught up with us.

He really took Jacob to task for sneaking off without letting him say goodbye to his daughters and grandchildren. I think he might have killed Jacob on the spot, except that he told us that, the night before, God had warned him in a dream not to harm Jacob. Jacob recited his list of grievances — how he had served fourteen years for his wives, and six for his flocks, and how Laban was always changing the terms to his own advantage. My father admitted it was all true. Then Laban asked Jacob why he had stolen his household gods, and Jacob, in all innocence, told him to search all the company, go into all the tents, and if he found them, the one in whose possession they were would be put to death at once.

Jacob did not know that I was the one who had stolen the gods. I had seen my chance to revenge myself on my father at last. According to the custom, whoever has possession of the gods is head of the tribe. They are evidence of a man's leadership and his claim to his property. Without them I knew my father would feel quite defenseless. As for me, I had long since accepted Jacob's Yahweh as the one true God. I knew those little clay figures had no divine power in them.

Laban searched and searched and finally came into my tent. I was sitting on the idols, which in itself is an act of disrespect to them. Cool as a cucumber, I said I hoped my father would excuse me from getting up, since it was that time of the month for me. He nodded and searched the tent thoroughly, but found nothing.

So Jacob and Laban made a covenant. Laban gathered stones together and made a heap of them, and Jacob set up a pillar. Jacob promised he would never mistreat either of Laban's daughters, or take other wives. Laban promised he would not pursue us further or make more claims on us. Then they said, "May the Lord watch between me and thee when we are absent, one from the other," and they called the place Mizpah, from the covenant they had made. We all ate together, and the next morning Laban kissed us and blessed us, and we went our separate ways.

So we traveled slowly the long, long miles back to the land from which Jacob had come. At first he was happy at the thought of seeing his parents again, but the nearer to Canaan we came, the more nervous he became about meeting his brother Esau again. He began to worry lest Esau make war on us, and began devising strategy. He would divide us into two camps. He would send many gifts ahead. He would put the maids and their children first, followed by Leah and her children, and last of all, Joseph and me. At last the scouts told us that the next day we would arrive within sight of the place where Esau was camped.

Now Jacob had never been a deeply religious man. He had inherited his father's and grandfather's faith. God had obviously guided him and protected him, but Jacob had never given himself to God, never humbled himself before God. Now on this last night he could not sleep. He left the tent and went out by a river. I was worried about him and followed at a distance. All night he seemed to wrestle with God, and I heard him pray that God would protect us all. Finally he prayed, "O Lord, I am not worthy of the least of all the steadfast love and all the faithfulness which thou hast shown to thy servant (Gen. 32:10).

So great was his struggle that God humbled him and for the rest of his life he limped, bearing in his body the mark of his encounter. Now Yahweh truly became the God of Jacob, as he had been the God of Abraham and the God of Isaac. And my Jacob became even more beautiful in his new humility and faithfulness. People recognized this in him.

Morning came, and we moved on and came nearer Esau's camp. He seemed to have about four hundred men with him, and Jacob's fear returned momentarily. Then we saw Esau running out alone to meet Jacob. It was beautiful to see him embrace Jacob warmly, weeping for joy to see him again.

(Blessings on our mother Rebekah for having sought his forgiveness and for having loved him and understood him so that he was no longer hurt and angry. How we wished she might have been present to see this reunion of her sons. But she had not lived to see this day, despite her hoping.) Isaac's faith had kept him alive, and he was there to share this happy reunion. He had gone blind, and so he had to be told what was happening.

One of the bonds between Jacob and me had always been the fact that we were both younger children, sorely tried by our elder siblings, and always wanting to get the better of them. Seeing Esau and Jacob embrace each other made me long to make peace with Leah. I sought her out, and I asked her forgiveness for all the spiteful things I had done and said over the years. She threw her arms around me and asked my forgiveness, too, and we both wept for joy.

Leah and I are really sisters now, sharing the work and the care of the children, confiding in one another, having fun together, exchanging ideas. She's so much better at some things than I am, and I've learned so much from her. Now that we do things together, the work gets done so much more quickly and easily. How different our lives would have been through all these years if we had only loved one another and not been hateful and mean.

I know now that love is the greatest thing in the world. It is the only thing that cannot be taken from you. It is the only thing that can survive death.

We are on another journey now. When Jacob was a young man and fled from Esau, the first night out he had a dream. He saw a ladder reaching up to heaven and angels going up and down. He knew that God was in that place, but he was not yet ready to humble himself before God. Instead he bargained with God, as he might have bargained with Laban, that if God would take him safely on his journey, some day we would return and build an altar. He called the place Beth-el, the dwelling of God. We are on our way home now, having fulfilled that promise.

It is a most difficult journey for me. God has answered my prayer and I am once more pregnant. However, things are even worse than they were before Joseph was born. Without Leah to help now, I do not know what I would do. I have talked to the midwife, and she tells me she is sure it will be another son, but he is in the wrong position to be born. I know, without her telling me, that if the baby cannot be delivered naturally, the law says they must rip me open and take the baby from me. If that happens, I will die.

It is a hard thing to face, and I call my unborn son Benoni, which means "Child of My Sorrow." Jacob, who does not yet know how serious things are, calls him Benjamin, which means "Child of Good Fortune." I do not want Jacob to know yet. How good it is to have Leah to talk to now, when I do not feel I should confide in Jacob. Sometimes she holds me close and I cry and cry.

There are times when I cannot bear it that I will never see my Joseph grow to manhood. I mourn for all the years of his life that I will miss. He's still so young, still so vulnerable. And I mourn for my little Benoni whom I may never see, or hold to my breast, or rock to sleep. I know Leah will care for him tenderly, but he is *my* child, for whom I had to pay such a high price. Someone else will play the part in his life that is rightfully mine. He will grow up, never having known his mother. Greater love has no woman than this, to give up her life for her child.

There are times when I feel all the sorrow of the world concentrated in me. I feel the weight of all the lost children, all the bereft mothers, all the separated lovers. Rachel means Ewe Lamb, and I suffer for all the helpless slaughtered creatures of the world, innocently giving up their lives in agony. Sometimes I cannot bear all the hurt and pain of the world. And then I feel that God is suffering with me and I am part of God's anguish for the world. I feel the everlasting arms around me and am comforted. The love of God is stronger than all the pain and hurt of the world. It is stronger than death.

I want to die at peace with everyone. When I finish writing this, I will send for Leah, and give her our father's household gods. I hope she can find some way to send them back to Haran. I will ask her to send a message to him that I have forgiven him for what happened on my wedding night. I hope he will forgive me for stealing his household gods.

Yes, I shall die, and the tribe will go on back home without me. I shall be buried somewhere here in the desert, and not in the family tomb that Abraham purchased when Sarah died and where they sleep together, and where Isaac and Rebekah are also buried. But I know that Jacob will set up a pillar to mark the place of my grave, and I know that his love for me will never cease. Our story will be told to all the generations of our children, and part of me will live on in them. So all is well.

O my beloved children, do not waste your precious short lives in hatred and jealousy, in pettiness and violence. Be quick to forgive. Bear all things. Believe all things, as Sarah learned to do. Hope all things, like Rebekah. And endure all things. You will find that love will never fail you. You can go right forward, even down to the gates of death, if you have love.

# Lot's Wife
Background: Genesis 11-14, 18, 19

*Remember Lot's wife. Whoever seeks to gain his life will lose it, but whoever loses his life will preserve it.* [Luke 17:32-33].

Don't ask my name. You wouldn't remember it if I told you. No one ever calls me by my name. The Hebrews found my Amorite name difficult to pronounce, so they gave up on it. They just called me Lot's wife. Lot's tent. Lot's coat. Lot's sheep. Lot's wife. I'm just one more possession. Lot had a pet name for me that means Beloved. Terms of endearment seemed to come natural to him. But he's been distant now for some time, and if he speaks to me now, it's usually "Hey, you . . . ."

I grew up in the prosperous, walled city of Haran, one of the chief Amorite centers and the gathering point for caravans in all directions. Haran stands out on the horizon, and its outline is distinctive, for my people built houses shaped like beehives. My family lived in a comfortable house outside the walled part of the city. Haran had grown so rapidly that there were as many people living outside the wall as within it. Haran was a good place to live. Trade was heavy, the climate almost ideal, and the land fertile. My father was a trader, often gone from home for long stretches of time with his caravan. He had seen most of the world.

It seemed that people came from all over the world to Haran. We got used to hearing different accents and seeing different clothes and customs. Sometimes strangers stayed a few weeks while they replenished provisions for a caravan or rested from an arduous journey. Sometimes they found the place so congenial that they stayed for years, settled down, and became part of the city life.

When I was a girl, a whole tribe came and pitched their tents outside the city wall, not too far from where we lived. They had come from Ur in Babylonia, hundreds of miles to the southeast, and had been on the road many months. They had large flocks of sheep and goats and staked out space for them to graze farther out from the city. They paid rent for that and rented space for their tents. Their leader, an old man named Terah, seemed tired and ill when they arrived. They decided to stay for a time, hoping that rest and the mild climate would restore him. It was obvious he could travel no longer.

These people were Hebrews. They were somewhat clannish and did not mix much with other people. They were clean and decent, for tent dwellers. They did not cause trouble. When they traded for things they needed in the city, people found them honest and concerned to give good value.

Terah had two sons, Abraham and Nahor, and they each had families and servants, as well as herders for their flocks. They were a good-sized group. Terah finally died, and Abraham, the elder son, bought a cave in which to bury him. He set up an altar near their campsite, but there was no idol on it. Abraham was now head of the tribe. He was a commanding person, with great dignity and presence, and people respected him.

Abraham's wife, Sarah, was very beautiful. They did not have any children of their own, but they had taken responsibility for Lot, a nephew of Abraham's whose father had died. Lot used to herd some of the flocks in the fields outside Haran. He was learning the business from Abraham. When he grew older, the flocks would be divided, and Abraham would set him up as a herder in his own right. I had charge of the few animals my family owned; I often saw Lot when we were both trying to keep track of stray sheep or goats. We became friends while we were still children, and as we grew older, we fell in love.

When Lot told his uncle Abraham that he wanted to marry me, he met with immediate resistence. Hebrews did not marry outside the tribe, Abraham told him. Lot protested that there was no one who was the right age suitable within the tribe. His uncle told him not to be impertinent and to get back to work and wait until the family could arrange a suitable alliance.

My family was not happy either. City-dwellers with a house, they thought it beneath me to marry a tent-dweller. They had better plans for me, they said — some nice Amorite boy from a prosperous family who would further my father's business interests.

We were in love, however, and we took matters into our own hands. When our families were presented with the fact that we were to have a child, there was nothing to do but let us be married. Of course both families complained loudly. My family was always polite to Lot, but they never really accepted him.

In Lot's family I was always to be the outsider. They never did see me as a person with a name, with dignity, with sensitivity. I was just Lot's wife.

Still we were happy: we had each other, and soon we would have our child. Uncle Abraham did divide the flocks with Lot, and now we had herders working for us and accounts to keep. It was fun living in a tent. Everything seemed like fun in the beginning.

Finally our baby was born. Lot was a bit disappointed that it was a girl, but he kept saying we would have many children and some of them were bound to be boys. I was secretly glad to have a daughter. When she grew older we would be able to talk and share our thoughts and feelings. I would tell her about my family and teach her about our people and our history. This way I would keep alive some of my own traditions and values. Had it been a boy, Lot would have given him a strong sense of being a Hebrew, and he would have seemed a little less mine. I still think everything would have turned out well for us if we had remained in Haran. I never quite realized how good life was there until I had to leave it.

One day Uncle Abraham called the whole tribe together. He told us that Yahweh, the Hebrew God, had told him to leave Haran to go to a land that would be shown to us. Yahweh promised Abraham that the Hebrews would be a great nation, and now we should go to lay claim to the land promised us. It is true that both the people and the flocks had been increasing; we were too many for the space being rented.

People asked many questions: Where was the land? How far away? Who lived there now? How would we know when we got there? Would we have to fight another tribe to take possession of it? Abraham had no answers for the questions. He just kept saying that Yahweh had told him to go and had promised to be our guide.

Nahor, Abraham's brother, grumbled that Yahweh had not told him to move on, so he was going to stay in Haran. Abraham agreed that he had a right to stay if he chose. I kept hoping Lot would want to stay also. I think he really did, but he and Uncle Nahor had never been close. His fortunes were tied up with Abraham. He chose to go.

I was very upset. True, I had known I was marrying into a semi-nomadic tribe, but the Hebrews had seemed so permanently settled at Haran I had thought they would stay forever. Now I was faced with leaving my family, my city, my world, my religion. There was not much likelihood that I would ever return.

My mother was too kind to say, "I told you so!" when I told her. She was upset too.

We held each other close and cried a long time. She did not see that I had any choice but to go with my husband. She gave me family things — some bowls and pitchers, and lovely pieces of jewelry that had come down to her from her mother; grandmother had been given them by her mother. Lot helped me pack them carefully. He was sorry I had to leave my family and my home, and he knew it was important to me to have things to pass on to our daughter.

Weeks of intense preparation followed. The men separated and divided the herds. The women repaired the tents and packed household things. Clothes were repaired and packed. Furniture and bulky things were sold in the market in Haran to provide money for the journey. Behind Abraham's back there was grumbling and apprehension. Where would we finally unpack things? How long before we would have a home again? It was hard to set out not knowing where we were to go.

Abraham thought the Promised Land would be somewhere in Canaan. He talked to traders in Haran about routes. We would head first for Damascus, several hundred miles away. That far the journey would be over a well-traveled road. Water and grazing land and places to camp would not be too hard to find.

Finally everything was as ready as we could make it. Abraham sent word around that we would leave early the next morning. Last-minute packing was done, and food was prepared to take along. I went for one last farewell to my family; I thought my heart would break.

Early the next morning Abraham lined us up and checked all the herds. We were quite a procession. Abraham walked confidently at the head and insisted on being cheerful. Most of us were not feeling light-hearted, and his cheeriness was annoying.

Our baby was growing. She was round-faced and the picture of health. She had begun to walk, but of course she would have to be carried most of the time on our march. She started out on Lot's shoulder, waving at the people lined up to say good-bye to us. Presently Abraham sent word back that he wanted to talk with Lot, and he handed her to me.

Our way lay gradually uphill and I found the baby grew heavier the longer I walked; I lagged behind. Near the crest of the hill, I had to stop to rest a bit, and I turned and looked back. Haran, my city, lay spread out before me. How beautiful it was with the sun shining on the white walls, illuminating the dear homely little houses. I shaded my eyes and tried to pick out my family's house. I thought of my wonderful mother. She would be grinding grain now. The tears came and rolled down my cheeks onto the baby's soft little head. I thought of each member of my family in turn. How dear they all were to me! I thought of the animals I tended, the individual sheep and the goats I had cared for. I thought of our neighbors, the girls I had grown up with, the children who played in the street near our house. What a wonderful community it was. Our lives are made up of relationships. How could I leave it all behind?

Leave-taking is a deep emotional need. I can attest to its necessity. And it takes time. I wept and wept there on the hill that showed me all my city for the last time. I could not go forward without that grief poured out.

Presently I heard Lot shouting to me. He had come back and not found me with the others, and he ran looking for me, panic-stricken. I saw him and knew then that I loved him enough to leave everything behind to go with him.

"I'm coming, Lot," I called.

Life on the road was hard. On a good day we probably made about fifteen miles. Other days we could not cover much distance. Every night a suitable place to camp had to be found. The animals had to be rounded up, watered, and allowed to graze. Tents had to be set up. Women had to get out utensils and equipment, grind grain, make bread, and cook over an open fire. Children had to be bathed and put to bed, and as the days followed each other, they became tired and often did not sleep well. And in the morning, the tents had to be taken down, and everything packed away again. Herds had to be rounded up and the whole company of people and animals assembled. I had discovered we were to have another child. My feet were swollen and hurt constantly. My back ached, and often I felt that I could go on no longer. Yet I had to keep on, day after day.

We met other caravans coming toward us on the road as we walked. Sometimes it was hard to keep their herds from getting mixed with ours. We asked each group we met how many days' marches they had come from Damascus. Slowly the number of days dwindled. We could look forward to our arrival there and to a breathing space. Abraham planned to sojourn several weeks there while provisions were restocked and inquiries made about the roads beyond. So far it had not been hard to find sufficient water and places to camp. Travelers on the road were often helpful to us in recommending places.

Finally we saw the towers of Damascus on the horizon. We hurried our steps and the herders prodded the animals. It took a while to find a suitable place to camp, for this was an even larger city than Haran and there were crowds everywhere. At last Abraham found a place, arranged for our use of it, and we set up our tents. It was good to be off the road for a time.

Abraham and Lot spent much time in the city. They learned that beyond Damascus water would be scarce and grazing land would be a problem to find along the road. There would be fewer travelers to give advice and so plans must be made carefully. Abraham learned as much as he could about where there were wells and springs in Canaan and how one got permission to use them. He still had no clear idea of where we were going, but he kept telling us that Yahweh would protect and guide us. I was skeptical. Would we find enough food along the way? We began to hear talk of wild animals and bands of robbers. I wondered where my baby would be born and how I would manage.

After several weeks Abraham once again told us to pack up and prepare to be on our way. After we left Damascus, we gradually left the fertile land and came into a hilly area. The rivers were all dry, and there was little for the herds to eat. We had to portion out what food we had and eat more sparingly. Some of the sheep died. Some days later we came into a desert region where food and water were even more scarce. We heard talk of famine from the few travelers we met. Even Abraham's unshakable faith wavered when day after day we found no food to gather or to buy.

Finally he told us that Yahweh said we should go to Egypt and sojourn there until the famine ended. I hoped I could hold out until we arrived in the fertile Nile valley, so that our new baby would have more chance of survival, but it was not to be. A small son was born prematurely one night. He only lived a few days; I had so little milk for him that he did not have a chance. We buried him in the desert. I thought my heart would break.

Our little girl had been so chubby and blooming with health when we left Haran, but week by week she grew thinner, and I feared lest we lose her too. We all counted the days until we should arrive in Egypt. As we came nearer, the roads were full of people, all headed for the fertile valley, all refugees like ourselves.

During our sojourn in Egypt, I lost faith in Abraham. Lot, too, lost some of the respect he had always had for his uncle. I still cannot understand how anyone who felt that he was called by God to found a new nation could have behaved the way he did.

Aunt Sarah was still a very beautiful woman, despite the hardships of our journey. Abraham was short of money to buy food. With the crowds that had poured in all trying to buy food, prices had gone up alarmingly. Abraham saw a way of building up his resources. Sarah had always acted like a princess and was something of a showoff. Abraham began walking around town with her and she attracted a good deal of attention. He told everyone that she was his sister, which was partly true: they had the same father, but different mothers.

Finally it all paid off. Scouts from the palace who were always looking for additions to the Pharaoh's harem noticed Sarah. She was taken to the palace to become one of Pharaoh's many concubines. Abraham was paid well. He acquired so many sheep, oxen, camels, even slaves, in return for his wife, that he became a rich man. He didn't seem to care what happened to her.

What happened next amazed me. Plagues descended on the palace. I should have thought Yahweh ought to have sent plagues on Abraham instead of Pharaoh, but I was glad he didn't, of course. Sarah was returned to Abraham and we were escorted to the border and told to leave the country. Abraham kept all the animals and slaves and money he had been given. I was appalled. We had no choice but to return to Canaan, and to hope the famine had abated. At least we had had a period of good food and were all feeling better.

Relations became strained between Lot and Abraham as a result of this unhappy incident. In addition, herds were constantly increasing and the herders had more work than they could handle. We were really too many to travel and camp together. A nasty quarrel broke out between the two groups of herdsmen. Lot had really wanted to go off on his own, and now Abraham saw the wisdom of going separate ways. He and Lot climbed the highest hill to be found near our campsite, and Abraham told Lot to choose which direction he would go, and Abraham would go in the opposite way.

Lot took him at his word. From the hilltop he saw the well-watered fertile valley of the Jordan River, and he chose that, leaving the dryer, less fertile land to his uncle. I felt a bit embarrassed that Lot should choose the obviously better site, after all his uncle had done for him. But Lot was not only disillusioned with Abraham; he was worried about his wife and daughter. I was pregnant again.

Abraham accepted the decision cheerfully. Again possessions, herds, servants were separated and divided. We said goodbye to Uncle Abraham and Aunt Sarah and headed East into the Jordan Valley.

We camped in easy stages without pushing. We both hoped we might find a place to settle down permanently. We knew there were cities in the valley, and we hoped we could find a good location near one of them. Lot knew how I longed for a permanent home of our own again. Both of us were weary of the uncertainty on the road. It was no way to bring up a family.

We covered about forty miles in a week, and found ourselves on the outskirts of a city called Sodom. We found a good place near a spring to camp and decided that we would stay. There was room for our flocks to graze, and the land was green. We could have a garden again and grow part of our food. Our days of being homeless wanderers would be over, and life would be good. We hugged each other with joy. Our little girl who had been so listless the last few weeks put up her little arms to us and said, "Me too, me too."

Lot went into the city to arrange for our use of the space, and we set up camp. Life settled into a happy routine. One day when Lot had been in the city to buy supplies, he came home in great excitement. He had found a little house available near the city gate and had arranged for us to move into the city. Our herders would continue to live in the camp outside the wall, but we would have a permanent home again, a real house. If only my mother might have known!

We moved our things into the house and I found places for
them. I got out all my family things that had been carefully
carried on our long journey. I hurried my arrangements for our
baby was due soon, and I wanted everything to be ready.

When my labor began, Lot ran next door and our wonderful
neighbor dropped everything and came to help. I was worn out
from many months on the road and did not have much strength
left. She kept encouraging me, and she rubbed my back to ease
the pain. She knew just what to do, and that gave me confidence.
After many hours our second daughter was born. If Lot was
disappointed, he did not show it. We had had a son — buried in
the desert — but now that we were settled, my strength would
come back. There would be more children, some of them sure to
be boys. Our girls grew and were healthy and happy and a great
joy to us.

Since we moved to Sodom, I have found myself part of a
wonderful support group of women, and I draw strength from
it every day. We care for one another's children. We help each
other out when there is sickness or when money is short. If a
calamity comes I can count on my neighbors. Our shed caught
fire, and the women all came running to help beat it out. But it
is more than just helping out in trouble. We share our joys, our
longings, our memories, our ways of doing things and of looking at the world. We talk about life and why we were born. We
speak of God, and we speak of death. We weep together and
comfort one another in times of grief and despair.

Unfortunately Lot has not found the men of Sodom so congenial. Their attitudes and values seem very different from
their wives' and from ours. The men drink heavily, and sometimes there are drunken brawls. They make coarse jokes about
their wives. Sometimes they visit prostitutes. They cheat in
their trading and then boast of it. They make money by paying
those who work for them too little to live on. They love to eat
and drink together and often overeat. Yet they turn aside from
crippled children begging a few coins on the street. Widows,
orphans, old people, the poor are no concern of theirs. Lot says
Sodom thrives on injustice and oppression and corruption (Isa.
1:10, 16-17; Ezek. 16:49).

Disasters have come, too. One year four kings of neighboring
cities who had been raiding in the valley advanced on Sodom.

Our king enlisted the support of four friendly kings of neighboring cities, and the battle finally took place just outside Sodom, uncomfortably near. In spite of outnumbering the enemy, our king and his allies were defeated. Lot had joined with the other men to defend Sodom, and he was taken captive along with the others.

One of our herders who witnessed the battle rode to Hebron, forty miles away, where we knew Abraham was sojourning. When he heard the news of his nephew's capture, he gathered about three hundred men and they set out immediately to rescue Lot. They arrived in the middle of the night and found the victorious kings sprawled around their campfire. They had been drinking in celebration of their victory. Abraham and his men completely routed them and rescued Lot and the other men of Sodom.

Lot came home to find that, in the midst of these terrible events, I had given birth prematurely to a little boy. He was beautiful and well-formed, and incredibly tiny. He only lived a few months and we buried him near our house.

The baby's death seemed to break Lot's spirit. He became discouraged and demoralized. He began drinking, and when he is drunk, he takes on the characteristics of the other men of Sodom. When he is sober, he is still the man I have always loved, but he also tends to be self-righteous and judgmental. He blames me now for failing to produce a living son. I've been unable to get pregnant again.

Our girls, who are growing into attractive young women, are afraid of him, for when he is drunk he is abusive and makes crude remarks. Sometimes he looks at them as no father should look at a daughter. He takes little interest in them, even when sober, except to criticize them. Sometimes I can reason with him, and he straightens out and is like the old Lot.

Sometimes he sits by the city gate late in the day to warn travelers that the streets of Sodom are not safe after dark. This evening he was sitting there when three men came up just before sundown. Lot warned them about Sodom and invited them home. We prepared a meal for them.

The men in town got wind of the strangers and gathered outside. They had been drinking and were armed with clubs and stones. They pounded on the gate, demanding that the strangers come out and identify themselves. Fearing for the safety of his

guests, Lot went out to reason with them. The mob was not to
be reasoned with, and Lot grew desperate.

Listening inside the house, I heard my husband, the father of
my children, offer his daughters to the mob in exchange for the
safety of three strangers. "Do to them as you please," he said,
"but spare the men who have come under the shelter of my
roof."

The girls cried in anguish. How could I comfort them?

The ordeal was not over yet. The mob turned on Lot. They
taunted him with being a mere sojourner in Sodom and then
self-righteously criticizing them. I was afraid they would kill
him and break down the door. Fortunately, one of our guests
had some kind of magic. He opened the door, pulled Lot back
into the house, and at the same time threw a powder at the men
that temporarily blinded them. The mob departed, but I feared
lest they return with reinforcements.

The girls are still sobbing. Lot has just come to us and told
us that our visitors are really angels. God plans to destroy
Sodom because of its wickedness. We must leave at once. He
tells me to pack a change of clothing for everyone and put
together some food. But what of our things? I ask. There is no
time to worry about them, he tells me.

Our guests come now and beg us to leave at once. I ask if I
cannot warn my friends and neighbors, but they insist there is
no time. Don't worry about Sodom, they say, for it deserves
destruction. I try to tell them about my friends, but they cut
me off.

Abraham dreams of the City of God, blossoming in the desert
of the Promised Land. I know a City of God right here, in the
midst of the wickedness of Sodom. How can God destroy my
kind neighbor next door? The elderly couple down the street?
The children who play outside our gate? How can I walk out
and leave my friends? How can I leave our baby's grave? My
family things? All that gives continuity and meaning to my
life? How can one go right forward without first taking leave?
I think I might stay and take my chances with the women and
children and the dumb animals of this beloved place. But no, if
I stay, what is to become of our girls? What will become of Lot
if I am not there to reason with him and love him and care for
him?

The first streaks of light can be seen in the east. The men

insist we must go now. I tell the girls and Lot to start on. I must pack one more thing.

I have cried so much. The tears are dried on my face, and my lips taste of salt. My clothes are damp. I feel like one of those strange salt formations that can be seen sometimes standing against the horizon outside the city. Some of them look like people. Perhaps they are women who turned back to take leave of some loved place doomed for destruction. Perhaps they had wept and wept until their tears dried and hardened, and they turned to salt. Salt is a strong preservative. In losing their lives, they preserved them.

Yes, Lot, I'm coming . . . .

# Miriam

Background: Exodus and Numbers especially
Exodus 1,2 and 15; Numbers 12, 20.

*For I brought you up from the land of Egypt, and
redeemed you from the house of bondage; and I sent
before you Moses, Aaron, and Miriam* [Mic. 6:4].

My name is Miriam. I grew up in Goshen (Gen. 45:10), the
Hebrew settlement in Egypt. The Hebrews, children of Israel,
had been in Egypt for four hundred years, ever since Joseph
had been the Pharaoh's deputy and his father and brothers and
their families had come in a time of famine. There had never
seemed any reason to return to Canaan, for the Egyptian climate
was ideal, the land fertile, the life good. At the time Joseph
came, the rulers of Egypt were another Semitic tribe, the Hyksos,
and they were friendly to us.[1]

Then the native Egyptians rebelled and overthrew their
foreign rulers. They reunited the country under an Egyptian
Pharoah, and things changed gradually for my people. Our
families had kept growing and our flocks increasing, so we
constantly needed more land than the original Goshen which
had once seemed so ample. Relations between Egyptians and
Hebrews grew strained.

Ramses II,[2] who was Pharaoh during my lifetime, had extended his empire and embarked on a huge building program.
He wanted roads to connect his vast kingdom, and magnificent
buildings to commemorate his reign. He needed cheap labor.
He had been uneasy about the large Hebrew population lest at
some time they unite with more hostile tribes to try to conquer

---

[1]Joseph and his brothers came to Egypt around 1650 B.C., during the
reign of the Hyksos Pharaohs, a Semitic people who had invaded
Egypt about 1710 B.C. and conquered the country during the Middle
Kingdom. Their kingdom included Syria and Palestine, as well as
Egypt, and lasted more than a century. It was a powerful rule and a
time of peace and prosperity. They introduced the horse-drawn
chariot and the composite bow. They were overthrown in 1550 B.C.
by Amasis I.

[2]Ramses II ruled from 1292 to 1225 B.C., a reign of 67 years. The
Exodus took place about 1250 to 1230 B.C.

Egypt again. He hit on the idea of using the Hebrews for his labor crews, and he made them slaves in the process.

I remember my father getting up before dawn when I was a child and laboring all day making bricks. It was hot, hard work; he came home after sundown and fell into bed exhausted. He grew old before his time and died when still a young man.

My parents were both descendents of Levi. The Levites had become the priestly tribe, and my father and mother were both devout. My mother, Jochebed, kept up the old family religious ceremonies that had come down from the time of Abraham the patriarch. When she invoked Yahweh's blessing, I had a sense of God's presence there in our humble house.

From childhood I was close to God. There is an ancient story from the time of Abraham that when the world was created, the Light of God came down to the earth in a clay jar, but the Light was so strong that the jar burst, and the fragments of Light became embedded in everything.[1] That is how I have seen the world much of my life, with the Light of God shining everywhere. I felt God had some special purpose for my life. When my father came home so worn out, telling of Egyptian overseers cruelly beating Hebrew slaves, I seemed to hear God say within me, "Comfort ye, comfort ye my people." I believed God would use me somehow to help bring our people to freedom, to the Promised Land of our ancestors where we could live in peace and justice and not be afraid.

Ramses II reasoned that if the Hebrew men worked hard enough, their population would decrease. His understanding of human nature must have been limited, for quite the opposite happened. There was something like a population explosion among my people during those bitter years. Pharaoh grew alarmed and ordered the Hebrew midwives to kill all the boys at birth. Our community was served by two wonderful women, Shiphrah and Puah, who had learned midwifery from their mothers. They simply ignored the order. Pharaoh sent for them, and with straight faces they told him that the Hebrew women were so strong and healthy that most of them had had their babies before the midwives could get there. Pharaoh

---

[1]This story is in the Cabala, which was said to go back to an oral tradition originating with Abraham. Actually we know now that it is much later in orgin.

apparently did not know much about delivering babies, and believed them. He decided on another course. He ordered all Hebrew baby boys thrown into the Nile. I've always admired Shiphrah and Puah. I hoped I could grow up to be as courageous and competent.

When I was seven and my little brother Aaron was three, our mother told me she was to have another child. She stayed inside most of the last half of her pregnancy and I ran the errands outside the house. She didn't want people to know there was another baby on the way. As her time drew near, she told me what would happen and how I could help. I had dreams of growing up to be a midwife like Shiphrah and Puah.

Finally my little brother was born. He was so beautiful, right from birth, that we all felt he was a special child. My mother and I fixed him a special place in our storeroom. We arranged the big storage pots of grain and vegetables so they hid the tiny pallet. I spent most of my time now caring for my baby brother, trying to soothe him so he would not cry.

Everything went well for about three months. Then one day he cried and cried; nothing Mother or I could do would quiet him. We knew now that we could not keep him hidden indefinitely. Indeed, after he calmed down, there was a knock at the door and an Egyptian inquired if there were a baby in the house. Mother calmly invited him to look around. He glanced around without going into the store room, and seeing nothing, departed, with the warning that if we were harboring a male infant he must be thrown at once into the Nile, or the whole family would suffer for it.

Jochebed and I both prayed to Yahweh to help us save our baby, and one morning I woke up with an idea. On my errands around town I had often seen the Pharaoh's daughter coming down to bathe in the Nile River with her handmaids. She looked like such a kind and friendly person, and once she had smiled at me, an unusual thing for an Egyptian to do to a Hebrew. My idea was that somehow we put our baby in the shallow water where the princess bathed, at a time when she might find him and rescue him. I was sure she would be moved to pity when she saw how beautiful he was.

My mother was skeptical at first, but the more she tried to think of alternatives, the better my idea seemed. She thought of using my father's fishing basket. She daubed it with pitch to make it waterproof, and I helped her line it with a soft little blanket. At the time when I knew the princess would be coming, we went to the river and floated our baby in his little basket near the shore. I kept watch behind some trees to see what would happen. I prayed that God would help me find the right words to say to the princess, and I prayed she might take pity on my small brother. The waves rocked the cradle slightly and the baby floated contentedly in his bed among the reeds near the shore.

Presently, the princess and her ladies came down to bathe as I had expected. The baby began to whimper. The princess looked around, saw the basket, and asked one of her maids to bring it to her. When she looked at the child she said, "Why, this must be one of the Hebrew children." She smiled at the baby, and then she picked him up and held him close and talked to him. His fussing stopped at once. She laughed, and the baby laughed back and she hugged him close again.

I decided it was the right moment to speak. Very politely I went up to her and said, "Would you like me to find someone to nurse him so he won't cry again?" She smiled at me, and said, "Yes, go bring someone." God had indeed answered our prayers.

I ran home quickly and brought my mother. The princess said to her, "I can't have children of my own. I think I want to adopt this child and raise him as my son. Take him home and nurse him, and I will pay you. Then when he is weaned, bring him to me." She held the baby close for a moment again, and said, "I think I'll call him Moses, because I drew him out of the water." Moses means "to draw out."

So we took our little Moses home and my mother nursed him and cared for him and tried to prepare herself for the time when she must give him up to someone else. Each month she went down to the river bank, so the princess could see how Moses was growing. Each month the princess paid my mother for nursing the child. My father was too ill to work, and this now provided us with enough to buy food.

When Moses was about three he was weaned and it was time for him to go to the palace to be a prince. The princess asked my mother if she would come to live at the palace and continue to care for him, looking after his clothes and serving as his nurse. I was ten now and Aaron seven. We could manage to care for our father, and we had good neighbors to help out. So it was arranged.

My brother grew up thinking that Pharaoh's daughter was his mother and his real mother was his nurse. Jochebed came home from time to time to report to us and to leave money for food and other needs. We managed, and the years passed quickly. Moses was given the best possible education to be had anywhere in the world. He learned to read and write the complicated picture symbols called hieroglyphics. He learned Egyptian history and memorized passages of poetry and other classic writings. He learned to hunt and to excel at athletics, and he also learned the skills of war. He was found to have an aptitude for sleight of hand; one of Pharaoh's chief magicians took him as a special protege. Everyone recognized that he was very bright and learned things quickly. There was only one problem. He could not speak without stammering.

As a boy he rarely left the palace grounds except to bathe in the Nile, but when he grew older, he, with other princes, was taken to see the great roads and monumental buildings under construction. The other boys were impressed by the engineering skill that was involved in erecting the buildings and their grandeur. Moses saw the slaves toiling in the hot sun and the cruelty and contempt with which they were treated.

Later Moses told me that he had grown up assuming he was an Egyptian but had always had a sense of being different. One day he asked Jochebed, "Who are these Hebrew slaves, and why are they treated so cruelly?" She told him how the Hebrews had come to Egypt in the famine and how their descendents had been impressed into labor gangs. She tried to speak as unemotionally as possible. Moses was troubled. "Why do I feel such sympathy for them?" he asked. Then Jochebed decided to tell him the truth about his origin.

Moses told her he was relieved to know the truth. Someday, he said, he would do something to free the Hebrews from their slavery. Perhaps this was why God had spared his life and let him be raised in Pharaoh's household. Jochebed cautioned him not to act rashly, but to wait until God revealed to him how and when to move. Meanwhile he should learn all he could and not tell anyone his secret.

It's hard to wait when you are young, and Moses was impetuous. When walking by himself one day, he saw an over-

seer cruelly beating an exhausted slave. No one was around.
Moses knocked the Egyptian down and he fell with a thud.
Unfortunately his head hit a brick and Moses found to his
horror that the man was dead. He quickly buried him in the
sand.

The next time he was walking, he saw two Hebrews quarrel-
ing and told them they should live in peace with each other.
One of them sneered and said, "Who are you to tell us what to
do? Are you going to kill us like you killed the Egyptian?" So
the murder was known. Too late, Moses realized the wisdom of
Jochebed's advice. Now he would have to flee.

When Pharaoh learned that Moses was gone, he sent soldiers
to bring him back. Moses had taken off into the desert and was
far enough ahead that the soldiers had to give up finding him.
For many years we did not know what had become of him.
Mother had to leave the palace, of course, and came home sick
at heart over what had happened. We all worried about Moses.

Aaron and I were grown now. Aaron, I am sure, was just as
bright as Moses. If he could have had an education, there
would have been no limit to what he might have done. Aaron
had the gift Moses lacked: he was a gifted speaker. His
eloquence was very persuasive.

Nor had God left me without a gift. Often in dreams I was
able to tell the meaning of events and to foresee what was to
happen. People came to me to interpret their dreams, just as
they had come to Joseph long ago. I prayed that I might always
be humble about my prophetic gift, and that I might always
use it to do God's will.[1] Now I began having dreams about
Moses. In the first I could see him trudging across the barren
desert, hot and thirsty, finally coming to an oasis with water
and trees. In another, I saw people living near the oasis, herders
like our people. They made Moses welcome. Later I had a dream
in which Moses seemed to be married and living with an
extended family. He was holding a little boy on his lap, and I
knew it was his child. I prayed then that God would reveal to
me where the oasis was located. That night I plainly saw the
desert, the oasis, and a very high mountain rising in the background. Moses and another man seemed to be praying at the

---

[1]Miriam is the first person in the Bible to be identified as a prophet
(Exod. 15:20).

foot of the mountain. Somehow I knew this was Mount Horeb.[1]

I told Jochebed and Aaron my dream. Aaron made inquiries about the best route to Horeb and learned it was about three days' journey. He determined to find Moses. I wanted to go too, but neither he nor Jochebed would hear of it. I helped pack food and water for his journey, and he set off.

Aaron did find Moses at the foot of the mountain. Was it chance that brought him there at that moment, or was it God? Moses was shaken from an encounter with God. He was herding his father-in-law's sheep and had come to the mountain intending to pray. He had seen a bush burning, but somehow the bush was not consumed. He went nearer to look, and God spoke to him and told him to take off his shoes, for he was on holy ground.

God told him it was time for him to return to Egypt and deliver his people from their bondage. Moses protested that he was inadequate for the task. God reminded him of all the great magic he had learned in the palace: how he could turn sticks into serpents and simulate leprosy. God told him he would teach him even greater magic that would persuade the Pharaoh to let his people go.

Moses still held back, saying that his speech impediment would be a hindrance in persuading Pharaoh. God became impatient and said, "Your brother Aaron is a fluent speaker, he will speak for you. See, here he comes now." Moses turned around and saw another man standing there. He did not recognize Aaron at first, nor was Aaron sure this was his brother. It had been many years since they had met, and both had been children at the time.

Moses took Aaron home to meet his father-in-law, Jethro, a Midianite priest and a wise and generous man. And Aaron met Jethro's seven daughters, including Zipporah, whom Moses had married. Aaron told them how I had dreamed of Mount Horeb; God had revealed where Moses was sojourning. Then Moses told about his encounter with God and how God had told him he must return to free his people. Jethro agreed that Moses must go back to Egypt and urged him to bring his people out to Horeb. There was room, water, and grazing land. Moses took leave of his family and the two brothers returned home.

---

[1]Also called Mount Sinai.

Our family was reunited for the first time since Moses had been a small boy.

Moses, Aaron, and I all shared how each of us felt called by God to help liberate the Hebrew people from bondage, and how each had been given a different gift: Moses his education, his training in leadership skills, and his magicianship; Aaron his eloquence; and I the gift of prophecy. Together we were more than we were as individuals. We needed one another. Together we planned the campaign against Pharaoh.

Moses and Aaron would go to the palace and ask Pharaoh to let the Hebrews go three days' march into the desert to make sacrifices to their God at Mount Horeb. I foresaw that Pharaoh would refuse and make things harder for the Hebrews, requiring them to gather their own straw for making the bricks. If that happened, Moses would bring a great plague on Egypt. He would turn the water of the Nile into blood, and all the fish would die. I foresaw that Pharaoh would temporarily relent, but then change his mind, once Moses called off the plague. Moses would have to produce more plagues.

And so it happened. Moses did turn the Nile to blood, and the fish did die. Pharaoh agreed to let the people go, and then changed his mind when Moses once again had restored the Nile to its normal purity. One by one, Moses called down the plagues: frogs, mosquitoes, gadflies, and then a cattle disease that killed the livestock. Each time Pharaoh relented, and each time he changed his mind. Then Moses conjured up a dust that gave people boils; then the hail came, and after that, the locusts. Still the familiar pattern: relenting and then hardening the heart.

While Aaron and Moses were occupied at the palace, I went quietly among our people, telling them what was happening and urging them to get ready to leave on short notice. They should sell what they could, pack what they could carry, and get food ready for the journey.

On the day of the worst and final plague, I told the women that they were to prepare a roast lamb over a campfire and that they should take some of the lamb's blood and smear it on their doorposts. That night the angel of God would kill all the first-born sons, but if their doorposts were marked, the angel would pass over the Hebrew homes. They would leave this night. There was no time for bread to rise; they would have to eat their roast lamb with unleavened bread.

That night when Pharaoh found his eldest son dead, he cried to Moses to take the people and go. After a hasty meal of roast lamb and unleavened bread, we all left quietly and headed eastward toward the desert. There were about three thousand of us who departed under cover of darkness, along with our animals.[1]

Yahweh told us not to go by the most direct route to Mount Horeb. We were to go in a round-about way so as to confuse Pharaoh's army who would undoubtedly pursue us. On the third day, we made camp on the shore of an arm of the Red Sea. It was a shallow place, full of reeds and mud. Moses sent out scouts, and they brought back word that the Egyptian army was indeed in pursuit. People panicked. The three of us had a hard time calming them down, telling them that the God who had led us thus far would not desert us now.

Moses stretched out his hand, and at once a strong east wind came up. It blew the shallow water into a wall, leaving the bare bottom exposed. Quickly we urged people to cross to the other side, and the last people climbed up on the opposite shore just as the first of the soldiers rode up. They shouted for the other troops to hurry and started to cross after us.

Their chariot wheels became mired in the mud. The horses thrashed around, and they, too, were stuck in the mud. The wind died down and the water returned. As we watched from the safety of the far side, the water grew deeper and deeper. The whole army perished as we watched.

Anxiety turned to incredulity and then to joy. We were free at last! I pulled my tamborine from my shoulder pack and began to dance and sing in exultation. All the women joined me, some of them with instruments. We danced and sang our gratitude to God and the words just poured out of me:

> Sing to the Lord, for he has triumphed gloriously;
> the horse and his rider he has thrown into the sea!
>
> [Exod. 15:21]

The children joined us and then the men. More words kept coming as we spontaneously celebrated our deliverance on the far shore of the Red Sea.

---

[1]Exod. 12:37 gives the figure of six hundred thousand men, not counting the children, but this is obviously an exaggeration. Scholars think three thousand is a more likely figure.

At last the dancing slowed. We turned our faces southward in the barren Sinai peninsula. For three days we marched, and we found no water. People complained again: why have we come out into the wilderness to die? How often they were to lose heart and complain in the years to come!

On the third day we reached an oasis, but joy turned to disappointment. The water was so bitter that people could not swallow it. Moses had lived in the desert for years, and he knew what to do. He found a small tamarisk tree, pulled it up by the roots, and threw it into the spring. At once the water became less bitter and soon was drinkable. We stayed several days there to rest and then pushed on again. A man alone can make Horeb in three days, but a motley group of three thousand with children and herds did not cover much ground in a day.

Before we reached Horeb, food ran low, and the people complained bitterly. God sent strange food which we called *manna*. When the dew dried in the morning, there was a fine flaky substance on the ground, looking something like coriander seeds and tasting like wafers made with honey. The people grew tired of this, however, and complained that there was no meat. We had meat to eat in Egypt, they said. God sent a flock of quail, and there was so much meat people became tired of it.

Every evening Moses, Aaron, and I gathered in a tent and talked over the events of the day and then planned as much as we could for the next day. We brought different points of view, and together we were wiser than any one of us alone.

Finally we saw Mount Horeb on the horizon. We would stay here for a long time, we had decided. Everyone was exhausted from the tension of the last days in Egypt and the hardships of the desert. We all needed time to rest and regain strength. We badly needed to organize people if we were ever to find a permanent home again in Canaan, the land God had promised our people centuries before.

Moses knew the situation in Horeb well. His father-in-law was helpful and wise; his advice and counsel would be invaluable. Moses also looked forward to seeing his wife and sons, Gershom and Eliezer. He talked more of Jethro, his father-in-law, than of his own wife and children, but when we arrived it was a joyful reunion. Aaron and I found Zipporah a strange woman, quite unlike her friendly, helpful father.

After a good night's sleep, we set about organizing people.

We decided that the descendants of each of the twelve sons of Israel should set up their own tent village. The twelve villages would be spread out in a huge circle; in the middle there would be a place for meetings. Each village would plan its food and water supply and stake out its grazing area. Tents needed repairing, and sheep needed shearing. Women and men both set to work.

God had given me a practical gift. I had a feel for where water was to be found. I worked with each tribe, helping people locate a sufficient source of water for their needs. I also gave advice on planting grain, lentils, beans, and certain herbs.[1] I searched out bark, berries, and other plants that had healing properties. People sent for me when they were sick, and I helped deliver more babies than I can count. I often thought of Shiphrah and Puah who had not survived to come with us. I found strength when I remembered their courage.

Inevitably quarrels arose, and Moses judged disputes with great wisdom. Somehow we had thought people would be less quarrelsome once we were settled again, but it was not so. There was no end to the judging, and Moses became exhausted. His father-in-law suggested he appoint responsible people in each tribe to judge the petty quarrels, and only the major problems should come to Moses. This system worked well, and Moses became easier to live with again.

We often talked about this in our evening consultations. Moses felt that if there were a general set of rules that would apply universally, people would not get into so much trouble. We talked of making up such rules ourselves, but finally we knew we needed commandments laid down by God himself, if this were to work. We prayed, and we decided that Moses should go up onto the mountain and ask God's help.

He set out one day, and the sky was overcast. Before long a storm came up, the rain beat down, and thunder and lightning echoed and played around the mountain top. Aaron and I felt it was a symbol that God was truly there. It must have taken courage for our brother to go on alone into God's presence,

---

[1]According to legend Miriam taught people to dig for water, till the ground, and cultivate trees. Clare Benedicks Fischer, Betsy Brenneman, and Anne McGrew Bennet, eds., *Women in a Strange Land* (Philadelphia: Fortress Press, 1975), p. 118.

when God was revealing himself so awesomely.

Days and days went by and still Moses did not return. The new moon came, grew full, waned and became new again: still he did not come. Through my dreams I knew he was talking with God at great length about our people, and I tried to reassure the others. They were sure he had died and would never come back. "Moses brought us out into the desert and now has abandoned us," people complained. Even Aaron began to lose faith, despite my reassurances.

The men came to Aaron and told him they needed a god they could see when they prayed. "It is hard to pray to Yahweh when you don't know what he looks like." they said. "Make us a god we can see like the Egyptian gods," they begged.

Aaron put them off for a time, but they were insistent. I labored long and hard with him, telling him that our God was too great, too vast, too deep, too high to be portrayed in anything tangible. I knew Moses would return, bringing God's commandments.

Aaron, however, was having to deal with the men who were getting desperate and were threatening him. Finally he told them to bring their earrings and bracelets and gold coins. He melted them down and made a golden calf. The people were delighted. The cow gives milk — a symbol of life and a good image for God. They began to sing and dance around the golden calf. Aaron built an altar and proclaimed a feast the next day. I stayed in my tent. This was an insult to the great God who had delivered us from bondage.

In the midst of the celebration, Moses finally came down the mountain, carrying two stone tablets on which he had written down the ten commandments God had given him on the mountain. He was angry when he saw the golden calf and he threw the tablets onto the ground. They smashed into a thousand pieces. Then he seized the idol and smashed it. People sneaked away. He melted the idol down and ground the gold into powder. He mixed it with drinking water and the people had to drink it. They were very contrite and asked his forgiveness.

Moses told them it was God's forgiveness that was needed. He would go up on the mountain again and ask for it. Perhaps God would forgive the people and dictate the commandments again. He warned that no matter how long he was gone they were not to lose faith and fall into sin again.

Moses was gone another forty days. God did give him the commandments again. What great wisdom lay in them — all that we needed to make life peaceful, orderly and just:

We were to worship only the one God, Yahweh.

We were not to make idols.

We were not to use God's name thoughtlessly.

We were to give every seventh day to rest and worship.

We were to honor our parents.

We were not to kill anyone.

We were not to desire another's husband or wife.

We were not to steal.

We were not to bear false witness.

We were not to covet another's possessions.

God also told Moses to make a portable sanctuary so that our God would be with us when we left Mount Horeb. It was to be a richly embroidered, colorful tent with poles of acacia wood. It was to be set up with an altar in front just outside the camp. Inside the tent was to be a small wooden chest called the Ark of the Covenant; it would contain the tablets on which the commandments were written.

The men made the tent poles and the gold and silver utensils for the priests to use at the altar. The women wove fine linen and embroidered it with beautiful symbols. Aaron and his descendants were to be the priests who made the sacrifices at the altar.

Aaron and I both noticed a change in Moses after the two periods on the mountain. Increasingly he made decisions without consulting us. He seemed to think he was the only one to whom God spoke. Aaron and I were hurt, for both of us had dedicated our lives to God, and we had often received messages from God which experience proved to be genuine. The three of us continued to meet each evening, but often Moses was late, or he left early; sometimes he did not come at all.

The three of us did decide that we should move on and go to Canaan, the land promised to our ancestors Abraham, Isaac, and Jacob. It was time to find a permanent home and end our nomadic days. After much discussion, Zipporah decided that she and her boys would remain with Jethro. She and Moses had little in common, especially now that he had face-to-face encounters with God on the mountaintop.

We all assembled by tribes, our goods and tents packed and

ready for travel, the animals rounded up. Priests carried the Ark of the Covenant at the head of our line. We felt that God blessed our journey northward to our homeland.

Much dismal wilderness and desert lay between us and the Promised Land, however. We camped at several places for fairly long stretches of time. The people kept on complaining; Moses became discouraged and weary of their perversity. He had left his family behind, and was, to some extent, cut off from Aaron and me by his choice. There was no longer the intensely close bond among us there once had been. Aaron and I grieved for him in his loneliness but were unable to reach him now.

We discovered a great deal of traffic through the desert now. We frequently met other tribes and solitary travelers, and sometimes we camped at places where other groups were sojourning. One evening we came to an oasis and found a small caravan of Cushites already camped there.[1] In the evening when we sat around our campfire, some of them came and we talked. They were much darker skinned than we and strangely beautiful. They were well-educated and well-traveled cosmopolitans like the Egyptians. Moses relaxed as we talked and seemed at ease with himself for the first time in many weeks. We had not realized how weary he must be of the uneducated, narrow-minded, complaining nomads he was leading. Even Aaron and I who shared much with him lacked the education to discuss world affairs.

The most articulate of the Cushites, and apparently their leader, was a strikingly beautiful woman. She was no longer young, but rather at the height of her powers. She wore bright clothes that set off her black skin, and we could not take our eyes off her. She was as well educated as Moses, the first such person he had seen in years, and they gravitated to each other. The rest of us fell silent and listened to the two of them discuss a wide range of subjects.

Days went by and each evening the gathering around the campfire took place. Aaron and I became a bit alarmed. Moses

---

[1]Cush was in the area of the Sudan. This whole section of East Africa south of Egypt, including present-day Sudan, Somalia, and Ethiopia, was often referred to in later Biblical times as Ethiopia. Many scholars think the "Cushite" wife of Moses is Zipporah the Midianite. I have chosen to take the Bible literally at this point, and assume a second wife from Africa. See Introduction.

was beginning to act like a young man in love, not like the responsible leader of thousands of people. There was nothing Aaron and I could do about it. Moses and the Cushite woman were married. She left her caravan and joined us.

Now all hope of re-establishing the tri-partite leadership we had once had was gone. Moses no longer bothered to come to Aaron and me in the evenings; he was much too involved with his beautiful wife. Matters that should have been taken care of went undone, and people began to complain. They were not happy that an outsider now absorbed most of the time of their leader. She could get away with not following the rules, when others could not.

One day Aaron and I cornered Moses and complained bitterly about his marrying outside the tribe and about his having cut us out of the leadership. "Has God spoken only through Moses?" we asked. "Has he not also spoken through us?"

I do not know whether what happened next was some trick of Moses or the working of God. Moses had learned ventriloquism among his other magical skills and occasionally used it with recalcitrant people. A voice called the three of us to the tent where the Ark was kept. A cloud came down and covered the entrance to the tent. A voice made it clear that God might speak to Aaron and me in dreams but that he spoke to Moses face to face.

When the cloud lifted I was stunned to find that I was completely leprous. We had occasionally seen Moses perform this trick before, and Aaron and I both assumed that he had done it. I was too appalled to speak, but Aaron cried out in great distress, "We may have spoken foolishly, but do not let our sister be as one who is dead." Dear loyal Aaron! Even Moses seemed a bit shocked as he looked at me, and he cried out to God, "Heal her, I beseech thee." Again the voice spoke, saying that I should be shut out of the camp for seven days and then could return.

It is a terrible thing to be treated as a leper, to be cast out of the community one has tried to serve loyally and unselfishly all one's life. It is a terrible thing to be cut off from human love and comfort, but it is even more terrible to be cut off from God. My whole life had been dedicated to God. Why was I punished and not Aaron who had also complained to Moses? Aaron came each night with food, but even he was afraid to put his arm around me and comfort me, for the whiteness of my leprosy shone in the night.

Then, when all help was gone, all hope was gone, in my loneliness and wretchedness, forsaken by my people, there under the night sky I found my God again. It was not the God of vengeance, not the God of justice and rules, but the God who suffers with us, who bears our griefs and carries our sorrows. He comes when all else is gone. We are never forgotten, never forsaken, never alone.

It no longer matters that Moses has cut Aaron and me out of the leadership. It no longer matters that I will not live to see the Promised Land. It no longer matters that people I have helped in their times of extremity now avoid me. It no longer matters that my body is old and tired from long days of hard work and long years of wandering in the desert.

We have come now to a place called Kadesh, a pleasant place with ample water. The oasis is within sight of southern Canaan. We will camp here while Moses sends men to spy out the land we hope to have for our home, but I will never leave Kadesh. I will die and be buried here.

A new generation has grown up and will claim the Land of Promise. They can go right forward because of the fortitude and the courage of those who started out from Egypt nearly forty years ago. It is enough that I have been part of this struggle for freedom.

I find myself praying:

> Lord, thou hast been our dwelling place in all generations.
> Before the mountains were brought forth, or ever thou hadst formed the earth and the world, even from everlasting to everlasting, thou *art* God.
> Thou turnest man to destruction; and sayest, Return, ye children of men.
> For a thousand years in thy sight are but as yesterday when it is past, and as a watch in the night.
> . . . . . . . . . . . . . . . . . . . . . . . . . . . . . . . . . . . . . . . . . . . . . . . . . . . . . . . . .
> So teach us to number our days, that we may apply our hearts unto wisdom.
> Return, O Lord, how long? and let it repent thee concerning thy servants.
> O satisfy us early with thy mercy; that we may rejoice and be glad all our days.

Make us glad according to the days wherein thou hast afflicted
us, and the years wherein we have seen evil.
Let thy work appear unto thy servants, and thy glory unto
their children.
And let the beauty of the Lord our God be upon us: and establish thou the work of our hands upon us; yea, the work of
our hands establish thou it.

[Ps. 90:1-4, 12-17 KJ]

# Tamar

Background: Genesis 38

*Then Judah . . . said, "She is more righteous than I . . ."*
[Gen. 38:26].

My name is Tamar, which means Date Palm. The trees are a familiar part of our landscape — tall against the skyline and much prized for their sweet fruit. Dates are an important part of our diet. My mother used to say to me when I was a child, "Be like the *tamar* and sink your roots into the living water so you will grow tall and bring forth much fruit."

During my long life I have learned to find strength deep within myself, for there was a time in my life when I felt betrayed; no one seemed ready to help me. I realized then that I would have to help myself and be responsible for my own life within the limits placed on women in our society. It was then I learned that when hope is gone, you can fall back on possibilities and keep yourself going day after day. You might say that "I dwell in possibility."[1]

I grew up in the Canaanite city of Adullam. Several hundred years ago, a nomadic desert tribe who called themselves Hebrews decided that their God had promised them the land of Canaan. They waged fierce battles to take our land, and, in the process, destroyed some of our cities. Somehow they never took Adullam, and it has remained in Canaanite hands. We are close to Jerusalem, their principal city, however, and today there is much trade back and forth. You may see Canaanite and Hebrew bargaining and trading without much friction in the market place of Adullam. Adullamites feel that they must keep their wits about them when they bargain with Hebrews, for they are very shrewd.

Now that I think about it, it was strange that a Hebrew man named Judah actually settled in our town and lived in the same household with a Canaanite family. Judah went into partnership with a man of our town named Hirah. They raised sheep and goats together and built up a good business. Everything

[1]From Emily Dickinson's poem #657.

they did seemed to prosper. They respected each other and cared for their mutual families, and they always seemed to have fun together.

Eventually Judah married a woman of our people, called Bathshua. Judah treated her well and they always seemed happy. I often saw them when I was a child. My regular job in our family was to draw water from the well in the middle of town, and that way I came to know all the people of our village. Sometimes when Judah was alone, I noticed that his face was sad and his eyes had a far away look. He was always kind to me. Sometimes bigger people pushed me around and I lost my turn at the well; then Judah would come to my aid and help me draw up the water.

Judah and Bathshua had three boys. Er, the eldest, was a little older than I. I thought him very good looking and clever. He looked a lot like his father and was always friendly to people. Onan, their second son, teased me and sometimes pulled my hair. I tried to keep out of his way, for he was a bully. Shelah, the youngest boy, was a handsome child, quite a bit younger than the older brothers. Of all the young men in the town I liked Er the best. I used to plan my trips to the well when I thought he might be there. Sometimes I saw him looking at me, and then I felt myself blush and dropped my eyes. By the time I was old enough to begin thinking about marriage, I was in love, and I knew I would love Er as long as I lived. I hoped he felt the same way about me; gradually I realized that he did. His kind father must have sensed what was in our hearts, for he arranged for us to be married.

We were so happy those early months of our marriage. I prayed earnestly to Ishtar, our fertility goddess. I wanted so much to give my wonderful husband the proverbial seven sons which the Hebrews count as the greatest blessing. Er used to laugh at my piety. He was confused about religion. His mother worshipped Baal and the other Canaanite gods, but his father remained true to Yahweh, the Hebrew god. It seemed strange to me that the Hebrews had only one God, and a male deity at that!

Did Er's confusion about religion displease the gods? Or should I have prayed to the Hebrew God? The months went by and still we had no children. But the years stretched ahead for us, and we were both sure that some day we would have our family. Nothing could really lessen our joy in being together.

One night, however, Er came home early from the pasture where he had been herding sheep. His stomach was upset and his throat sore, and I knew at once that he was very ill. When I felt him, I realized his fever was very high. I stayed up all night bathing his head with cool cloths, and trying to make him comfortable. The next day he was worse, and I knew I might lose him. He lay with his head pillowed on my lap, and looked up at me and said, "If only we could have had a son, so that my name will not perish from the Book of Life . . ." I promised him that I would try to have a son to carry on his name, and that I would always love him. He looked up at me tenderly, and then he was gone. I thought my heart would break. I will mourn him as long as I live.

There is a law that the brother of a man who dies without an heir is to marry the widow. The first son of such a union is counted as the son of the deceased man, and so his name is carried on. I knew Judah would probably marry me to Onan, after the required time of mourning, and I contemplated this with mixed feelings.

I had never liked Onan and knew that he had no use for me. I did not think I could ever love him. I worried about the fact that he was often mean and petty. He was likely to be cruel, and wives have no recourse in our society when husbands abuse them. Life would not be easy as his wife. But I wanted so much to have a son for Er that I was willing to do anything, even live with Onan for the rest of my life. Er and Onan had never got along. Eldest sons have many privileges, and though Er was too nice to rub it in, I knew that Onan had always resented him and made his life miserable in little ways. I hoped he would change now that Er was gone.

In due time Judah arranged for us to be married. But right away Onan let me know that he had no intention of playing the role of husband to me. No way was he going to have a son to carry on Er's name and place in the family. My position became intolerable. I was married to a man who refused to give me children. Our marriage was never consumated.

Evidently Onan's behavior displeased the gods also, for within a year he also died of a sudden fever, just as Er had. I tried to nurse him as well as I could, but he resented my presence and said he would rather be alone. I confess it was a relief to me when the end came. My heart ached for Judah and Bathshua, however, who had lost two sons so close together. I mourned with them, for I loved them and had never had anything but kindness from them.

Judah told me to go back to my family and wait until Shelah, their youngest son, should grow up and be old enough to marry. Judah and Bathshua never reproached me or said anything in my presence, but I knew that they must feel that somehow being married to me had caused both their sons to die.

I had no choice but to go back to my mother's house in my widow's clothes. My father had died and it was a hard time for my family. They were not particularly happy to have me back. My clothes were depressing too, but respect for my two husbands required that I continue to dress as a widow. There was not much joy in life for me, or for my family. It was now that I had to put down roots deep within myself to find strength to endure. I often despaired that my life would ever bear fruit of any sort, let alone the sweet and valuable dates which finally crown the palm tree.

On trips into town on errands and to the well for water, I watched for Shelah. Month after month I noticed that he was growing taller, more mature, more handsome and sure of himself. Any day now Judah must give him to me in marriage. I longed to exchange "beauty for ashes, the oil of joy for mourning, and the garment of praise for the spirit of heaviness" (Isa. 61:3 KJ). I longed to put on wedding garments once more and establish a home and family with Er's beloved little brother now grown into promising manhood.

The months stretched into years and still no word came from Judah. I kept going to the well when I thought he might be there, so as to remind him by my presence of his obligation to his daughter-in-law, but I knew he was avoiding me. Finally I had to accept the bitter truth: Judah and Bathshua were so afraid of losing their last son that they would postpone indefinitely his marriage to me.

Then I heard rumors that Shelah had been sent off to visit some distant relatives and, later, that he had married one of his cousins. My despair and grief were overwhelming. How could I ever give Er a son to carry on his name? I prayed to Baal and I prayed to Yahweh, but no god inclined an ear toward me and answered my prayer.

I was going to have to work out my problems without divine or human help. My family considered me a burden. My husband's family had cut off contact with me. The townspeople avoided the widow and I knew they talked about me behind my back. They were ready to believe that somehow it was my fault that Er and Onan had died prematurely. The only person who still greeted me kindly was Hirah, Judah's friend and partner. He never failed to speak to me and sometimes passed on news of Judah and Bathshua.

So it was that I learned of Bathshua's illness and then her death. Judah was now in mourning for her. I remembered things Er had told me about his parents, and I was sure that Judah mourned his wife sincerely because he loved her. I also knew that he was mourning the absence of a warm and loving presence in his bed each night. My heart went out to him. I know what it is to ache with love and to have to sleep alone.

One day I met Hirah at the well and he told me that Judah's prescribed mourning for his wife was nearly over and that they would be going up to Timna together for the sheep shearing. A plan began to form in my head. If there were no brothers of Er to provide a son in his name, there was still someone else in the family who carried the same blood line.

Adullam has never had commercial prostitution. However, there are women who belong to the cult of Ishtar, the mother goddess, who have relations with men as part of a religious ritual. They are always heavily veiled because it is thought that Ishtar is really using their bodies, and their individuality does not count. Even though temple prostitution is rare in Adullam, now it seemed a possibility for the solution of my problems.

On the day that Judah and Hirah were to go up to Timna to shear their sheep, I took off my mourning clothes and dressed in bright garments with a heavy veil over my face. I was sure I could count on Judah's need. I waited near the temple at a place where I knew Judah and Hirah would have to pass. I was not ashamed of what I was doing. It was the fulfilment of my promise to my beloved husband as he died in my arms. How else could I give Er the longed-for son to carry on his name?

Things turned out as I had hoped. Judah approached me, assuming I was a cult prostitute. He obviously did not recognize me, even when I spoke to him. I asked him what he would give in return for my favors, and he said he would send a kid from his flock as a sacrifice to Ishtar. I asked him for some surety. Impatiently he asked what I wanted. Calmly I asked for his signet ring, the cord that held it around his neck, and his staff. He gave them to me without a second thought.

I knew Judah to be thoroughly honest. He would send the promised kid, but I did not intend to be around to receive it. Later I heard that Hirah had spent some time on Judah's behalf inquiring around town about the temple prostitute. But I had taken great care not to be seen by anyone but Judah and Hirah. People told Hirah that he should know there were no prostitutes in Adullam.

Before long it was evident to me that my prayers had finally been answered. By three months it was noticeable to other people. There was no way to keep people from gossiping in our town, so word reached Judah that his daughter-in-law had committed adultery and was expecting a child. In accordance with the law, he sentenced me to be burned to death.

I allowed myself to be brought before him without protest. Then when everyone was assembled to witness my execution, I said loudly and clearly: "I am with child by the man who owns these. See if you recognize whose seal and cord and staff these are."

My heart went out to Judah, for he is honorable as well as honest. Without hesitation he said, "She is more righteous than I, since I would not give her to my son Shelah." And so he publicly acknowledged his paternity. I took off my mourning clothes and returned to his household. We never slept together again. For many years now we have lived under the same roof, as father and daughter, in mutual respect and companionship.

It turned out to be a most difficult pregnancy. I felt I must be carrying twins, for I grew abnormally large. Judah told me about his grandmother, Rebekah, and how her twins, Jacob and Esau, seemed to be at war within her before birth, as they were to be in later years. It helped to know that someone else had survived such a violent pregnancy.

At last my time came and all my fears were realized. I doubted I would survive. One of the babies put out a hand, and the midwife grabbed it and pulled. She tied a red thread around it, signifying that this would be the first born, but her efforts to bring the child out were fruitless. The hand withdrew. Soon the other baby was born with a great struggle that I thought would tear me apart. The midwife exclaimed as she drew him forth, "What a breach you have made!" So we called him Perez, which means Breach. Finally the other child was born, with the scarlet thread around his wrist, so we named him Zerah, which means Scarlet, or Bright.

It took a while for me to recover, but in time my strength returned. Judah proved a good father to the boys, and our days were happy and peaceful. I have come to love him very much and have found him very companionable. It would have been nice to have a husband again, but it has been a blessing to share a home with Judah.

He often talked about his family, and I loved to hear the stories he told. His father was called Jacob, but Yahweh gave him another name, Israel. Jacob had two wives, sisters, named Leah and Rachel. Judah has a great tenderness for his mother, Leah, for Jacob did not love her in the way he loved Rachel. God rewarded Leah with six sons and a daughter to make up to her for the lack of her husband's affection. Judah was her fourth son. Jacob also had two sons apiece by the maids of his wives. Then finally, Rachel, the beloved wife, had a son who was called Joseph. Jacob loved the boy more than all his other sons and spoiled him. He became a show-off and a boaster; his brothers all disliked and resented him.

Judah told me how they plotted among themselves to get rid of Joseph. When the older brothers were all off with the flocks at a distant pasture, their father sent Joseph to find out how things were going and to bring them more provisions. When the brothers saw him coming in his beautiful clothes and his confident manner, they decided to kill him and pretend to their father that he had been killed by some wild animal. Only Reuben, the eldest, held out and said, "Let us not kill him." Finally Judah's conscience troubled him, and he suggested they sell Joseph as a slave to some traders whose caravan he saw approaching. That seemed like a lesser evil than murder, so it was done.

When they returned home, they were not prepared for the depth of their father's grief. The mourning went on and on. Jacob refused to eat for a long time and grew thin and haggard. He lost interest in everything; they feared for his life. Judah began to have bad dreams about what might have happened to

Joseph. Finally he could stand the tension no longer. He could not continue to live with his father on the basis of dishonesty, nor could he live with his brothers if he broke their pact of silence on what they had done. So Judah separated himself from his family and went to live with his friend Hirah in Adullam.

As he talked I realized that all this was still troubling him, so I urged him to return to his family. He and Hirah reluctantly dissoved their partnership and divided their flocks between them. Judah and I and our sons returned to his family circle. So it was that we lived through the famine, and the brothers went down to Egypt to buy grain. There they finally learned how Joseph had prospered and become the Pharaoh's deputy. The famine lasted seven years, and eventually Israel and all his family moved to Egypt.

Our boys are growing into fine young men. Er would be proud of them. My heart is full, for I was given not just one son, but two, for my beloved husband. And my life has been rich with Judah's companionship. Judah's God, Yahweh, has become my God too, and I feel now wholly part of what I have come to call Judah-ism.

I like to think of the strong, resourceful women in Judah's family and hope I may be worthy of them. I feel a kinship with them. Like Sarah, his great-grandmother, I had faith that I would have a child, though it seemed quite impossible. Like his grandmother, Rebekah, I had a difficult childbirth with twins. Like his mother and his aunt, Leah and Rachel, I have been zealous in love. And, like the date palm whose name I bear, I have grown deep roots and been blessed at last with good fruit.

Judah's people cherish a dream that one day the Messiah will come and bring God's peace to the world. Then brothers will live together in mutual understanding and love, and not be jealous of one another. All sons will be important, whatever their position in the family, and daughters will be cherished too. There will be no more slavery. Women will be valued as full human beings and will no longer be owned by their fathers and husbands. Then no one will be reduced to playing the harlot. But I think the Messiah will treat even harlots with respect. He will say to the men, "Let him who is without sin cast the first stone . . ." (John 8:7). Women, as well as men, will become followers of the Messiah, and when his enemies seek to destroy him, the women will be there, faithful even till death.

Dare I hope that one of my sons might be an ancestor of this Prince of Peace? It is a possibility, and in that hope I go right forward, year after year.

# CRahab

*By faith the walls of Jericho fell down, after they were
compassed about seven days.*
*By faith the harlot Rahab perished not with them that
believed not, when she had received the spies with
peace* [Heb. 11:30-31 KJ].

*... Was not Rahab the harlot justified by works, when
she had received the messengers, and had sent them
out another way?*
*For as the body without the spirit is dead, so faith with-
out works is dead also* [James 2:25-26 KJ].

I am Rahab. You might think that Rahab means Harlot, for
that is how I have been spoken of since I was a girl: Rahab the
harlot. Even after I married and had children by a legitimate
husband, people still called me Rahab the harlot. It's hard to
outlive one's past.

The Israelites, who are my people now, call sea monsters
rahabs. I've never been clear about the distinction between
rahabs and leviathans, but rahab has become for them a symbol of chaos, and even more specifically an epithet for Egypt,
their long time enemy and enslaver (Ps. 87:4, 89:10). I suspect
that my fellow Canaanites who lived in Jericho with me would
think of me as a monster — if they had survived to think of me
at all.

But sea monster was not what the word meant to my family
and to the midwife who gave it to me. Actually, rahab means
Wide or Broad; I was given the name because I was a chunky
little baby and my mother had great difficulty delivering me. I
was the oldest child to survive, and since food was scarce, I
needed that extra weight at birth.

Like all women, my mother kept on having children year
after year, giving birth to them with great trouble and having
less and less with which to nourish them. Some survived and
some didn't. Those who did were puny, and often not well. My
mother too grew sickly as the endless cycle of childbirth went

on. Since I was tough, I took much of the care of the house and of my younger sisters and brothers; my mother simply did not have the strength for hard work. She spent her days spinning, for it was a constant struggle to keep us all clothed. She taught me to spin and weave and our hands were never idle. Like most Jericho families we raised flax. The houses were all flat-roofed, and in the spring you could see the great stalks drying on all the roofs. They helped to keep the houses cool.

Jericho, my city, was built on a hill. It must have been very old, for you could find bits of ancient pottery and tools when you dug deep in planting the garden. I suspect that my ancestors lived in Jericho for hundreds of years. It was a walled city — the only important place in the southern end of the valley of the Jordan River. In the middle of town stood our King's palace. It was a two story building, but not too luxurious. Beside it was the temple of the storm god, Baal, whom we presumably worshipped; no one had much faith in Baal when I was a girl. We were all poor and demoralized. Everyone had to hustle to keep alive.

My father hustled too. He sold extra produce from our garden, though we ate most of what we raised, and he sold linen my mother made. He did odd jobs and ran errands for people, but he never earned enough to feed us adequately. We were often hungry. Eventually he grew lame and limped around on his errands. Gradually his joints became stiff. Finally he was paralyzed with arthritis. He could no longer work.

I was the only strong, able-bodied member of the family. Somehow I had to earn a living and keep the family going until some of my younger brothers could help. But I ask you, how can a woman earn a living? We are taught to be humble and meek and subservient. Humility has always seemed to me a rather nasty little virtue and not much help to a woman who has to support a large family.

My father had often sold vegetables and fruits from our garden to the woman who kept the inn at the city gate. Her house was built right into the city wall; it was one of the few two-story houses in town. From the second floor you could look out over the wall to the plain beyond, and on clear days you could glimpse the Jordan River. I had never been allowed to go to the inn; there were rumors that it was not a place for decent women to go.

But now, with my father unable to make his rounds, I peddled the produce and made the acquaintance of the innkeeper. She was friendly and sympathetic to our family problems. She always asked after my father. One day she asked if I would like to earn a little money. I jumped at the chance. She drew me inside and explained to me what she called "the oldest profession." And so I found a way to support my family.

I did not tell my family, so it was a while before they waked up to what I was doing. They had been so glad to have enough food that they had not inquired too closely as to how I came by the money to provide it. By the time they knew, I was already known as Rahab the harlot.

I learned to put on a very meek exterior and to accept quietly whatever was done to me. I came to despise the men of Jericho, however. They often were cruel and inflicted unnecessary pain; they treated me with contempt and made me the butt of their jokes. They were an evil lot, cheating on their wives with no pity for the young girl they were using. Beneath my humble exterior I was alert for every advantage I could take, every scrap of information I could pick up, and I learned to play one man against another to my financial advantage.

My employer was growing old, and she increasingly turned over to me the running of the inn, as well as what she called "service to the customers." She was not well, and she told me she would arrange for me to inherit the inn after her death. I became a business woman in my own right and could support my family adequately.

My standards were high for Jericho. Travelers received good food and wine for their money, and those who sought other favors received their money's worth. Business prospered even in those depressed times. Because I was strategically located right next to the city gate, travelers from all parts of the world stopped with me, and my inn became a gathering place for news. I was always humbly in the background, being accomodating, but my ears were sharp to learn everything I could. I was still the butt of jokes, but I was also now accepted, even respected in a way. I was often included in the all-male talk going on around me.

So it was that I learned about a desert tribe called Hebrews, nomads for decades, who were becoming a menace in the desert region across the Jordan. We heard that they had destroyed the kingdoms of two of the Amorite kings, Sihon and Og. Later we heard rumors that Moses, their strong leader, was failing, and, eventually, that he had died. They had never come near enough to us to be a threat. The Jordan River, wide and deep, lay between us and the desert.

Soon there were rumors that the Hebrews had a new leader, even more powerful than Moses. His name was Joshua, and he appeared to be assembling all his people in a camp across the river. Still, the men of Jericho reasoned, with our city walled and the river between us, there was no need to panic. Therefore no one bothered to repair the breaches in the wall or assemble stores and weapons in case of siege. The men continued to get drunk regularly, to buy my favors, and to spend their days in idleness and their nights in revelry. They all said, half-jokingly, "Baal will protect us." They said it without much conviction. I often wondered how they could be so blind and stupid.

One day two men came into the inn. I saw at once they were not the usual traders. They did not talk much, but called for drinks. I served them and they began to relax. I asked casually what brought them to Jericho, and saw a faint reddening beneath the sunburn of their faces. My heart quickened. I knew they must be spies. So Jericho was marked for destruction! Why else would they be here except to find out how vulnerable we were? They drank slowly, and when their cups were empty I asked if they wanted my services in an upstairs room. They politely told me that they had wives of their own to whom they were faithful.

This unexpected response unnerved me, and I burst into tears. One of the men reached out and patted me on the shoulder in a gesture of comfort. It was the first time in my life that a man had seemed to see me as a person with feelings, and not just a body to be used. I realized that no one, not even my family, had ever tried to comfort me. I was the strong one who did the comforting.

No one else was around. Quietly I told them that I suspected they were Hebrew scouts. I asked them to tell me why they were true to their wives, even away from home.

One of them introduced himself as Salmon. He told me about their God whom they call Yahweh. Yahweh had given laws for the people to their leader Moses in a face-to-face encounter on Mount Sinai in the desert. Yahweh had told Moses that there was only one God and that they should not make idols, nor profane Yahweh's name. One day a week was to be kept holy. They were to honor their parents, and they were not to kill nor to commit adultery. They were not to steal, bear false witness, nor covet their neighbors' possessions. I could hardly believe what I heard. Why, our stupid little Baal was no god at all. Surely this Yahweh must really be the only God in heaven or earth. I could give my heart to such a God.

Suddenly I became aware of people approaching in the street. I bolted the door and hurried the men up to the roof. I had them lie down and I covered them completely with stalks, so that there was no sign of them. It was getting late, nearly time for the city gate to be closed. The coming darkness would help to conceal the men.

Two soldiers were pounding on the door when I came down. They had an order from the king to take into custody the strangers who had been seen coming into the inn. Rumor had reached the king that they might be spies. "It is true," I answered calmly, "Two men did come in today, but I do not know from where. When I told them the gate was about to be closed, they left. If you pursue them, I am sure you can overtake them."

My years of humility paid off. They took me at my word and rushed out just as the gate was being closed. I ran upstairs and could see them riding off in the direction of the Jordan. I could hardly believe my good fortune. I had outsmarted the king's men!

There was no time to lose. Quickly I bolted the door again and ran up to the roof. I led the men down to the second floor, and they shook the bits of flax stalk out of their hair and clothing. I told them that I knew their God had promised them our land, and I assured them that Jericho was ripe to be taken. I told them the wall was not in very good repair. I said the men were not well-trained and disciplined, and that while they were fond of boasting, they really were not very courageous. Salmon smiled and said that perhaps the Jericho women made up for the men's lack of courage, if I was an example.

I asked them, then, to swear by their God that in return for my protecting them now that they would guarantee the safety of all my family when they took the city. They both promised, "Our life for yours, if you do not tell our business. When Yahweh gives us the land, we will deal kindly and faithfully with you and your kin." They told me that when I observed the city was about to be taken, I should gather all my family at the inn and bind a scarlet cord in the window.

Now I let them down through the window on the outside of the wall. It was quite dark and they would not be seen. I suggested that they remain in the hills for three days before returning to their camp, since I had seen the king's men riding toward the Jordan. Two days later the king's men rode back into town. They had searched and found no trace of the men, of course.

Every day I went up to the roof and tried to figure what the Hebrews were doing and how and when the siege of Jericho would begin. Joshua gave orders to break camp, I noted. Yahweh was with them, for I could see the waters of the Jordan seem to part in front of them as they crossed it, just as we had heard that the Red Sea had parted when they left Egypt. Once across the river they made camp on our side and set up twelve stones from the river in a circle. Later I learned that this symbolized the twelve sons of Jacob, founders of their twelve tribes. We still call that place Gilgal, which means circle. While they were camped there, they celebrated their annual Passover ceremony in remembrance of their years of slavery in Egypt and their delivery from bondage by Moses. They certainly seemed to be in no hurry to take Jericho!

Meanwhile the men in the city began half-heartedly to drill and to repair some of the sections of the wall. It was too little and too late, of course. Each day we expected the attack, and each day nothing happened. It got on our nerves.

Then one morning as the sun rose, we found that they were all gathered in front of the city gate in orderly fashion. Their priests were at the head of the procession, carrying a large ornamental box they call the Ark of the Covenant. (Salmon told me all this later.) The Ark symbolizes the presence of Yahweh. The Ark always goes into battle with them to remind them that their God is on their side and fighting with them. After the priests came the soldiers. They all stood there silently. Then at a signal, they marched completely around the city, without a sound. Then they withdrew to their camp on the river. What did it all mean?

Six days in a row they did this. The tension grew greater each day in the city. We would have understood an attack, but this silent procession was ominous. My family had long since assembled at the inn, and we all watched intently.

On the seventh day, they made their usual circuit of the wall and then repeated it six times. On the seventh round, the priests suddenly blew loudly on their trumpets and all the Hebrew soldiers let out a blood-curdling yell. The attack had finally begun. What had I to lose now? I ran out of the Inn and with all my strength I managed to slide back the heavy bolts of the city gates to let them in. When I turned around, I saw the walls had fallen and the Hebrews were streaming in on all sides.

True to their word, the two men I knew were standing outside the inn window. They helped each member of my family down over the crumbling wall, and then I climbed down too. They led us beyond the battle headquarters to where the families were camped. We were fed and made comfortable and tents were made available for our use. Salmon's wife was especially helpful in comforting some of the frightened children in my family. We were treated as honored guests.

Now we watched from afar as flames rose from Jericho. We knew no one would live to escape, and by the next morning there was nothing left but smoking ruins. I could not mourn for the stupid god Baal, nor for the wicked men who had so often made my life miserable, but I was haunted by the remembrance of women and children. I remembered women who had helped my mother in childbirth; women who had sent in food when we had nothing to eat; women who had rubbed my father's stiff joints. I remembered the neighbors' children innocently playing with my brothers and sisters. I thought of the patient animals on whom we depended for milk, or wool, and the asses who carried our burdens on their backs. Did Yahweh not care about the innocent victims of war?

Why are the choices of life so difficult? Why must decisions never be clearly right or wrong? I had betrayed my city for a God more worthy of respect than the god I had known. I had given up my religion for a higher standard of behavior. After the immorality of the men of my city, the moral code of the Hebrew men had seemed so beautiful and so right. I had given up the life I had known for something that seemed "somehow strangely better." But why did the innocent have to perish with the guilty? I could not get the children of Jericho out of my mind; my sleep was troubled for many months.

Days went by. Everyone was kind to us, and life settled into an orderly routine. I could not regret being with them, for their way of life seemed beautiful to me. Salmon and his wife were especially kind. Often in the evening they sat and talked with us around the campfire. I asked many questions, trying to understand their religion and learn about their history. Salmon teased me about my insatiable thirst for knowledge. Before this kind and courageous man I felt truly humble, not falsely meek as I had always been. I began to think of humility as a willingness to learn, to become teachable.[1] So I kept on asking questions.

Gradually my heart began to heal, and one day it dawned on me that I was no longer Rahab the harlot. No man had sought to use my body, nor had anyone made jokes or obscene remarks about me. I regretted the terrible years of my bondage. I longed to be clean and worthy of marriage to some decent man. In my heart I wished Yahweh might give me a husband as thoughtful and kind as Salmon.

Months went by. The Hebrews conquered the land and our life became more settled. We had more permanent dwellings. Salmon's wife took ill, and after a time, she died. Now it was my turn to comfort my friend. As the days passed and his period of mourning ended, he continued to come in the evening to talk.

Gradually my heart's desire came into being. Friendship deepened into love, and finally we were married. I told him that from now on his people would be my people, and his God my God. In spite of all the abuse my body had taken, I came to know how beautiful the love of a husband and wife can be.

We settled in the little town of Bethlehem, and there our son, Boaz, was born. By now I was fully accepted as a Hebrew, and I knew I had the respect and love of everyone in the town. I worship Yahweh who is a greater God than any I have ever heard about, and I do believe he is the one God, the only God.

But I wonder why Yahweh told his people not to kill, and still condones their slaughtering of the innocent children in the cities they conquer. Salmon says not to worry about it, for this

---

[1] A Friend in California shared this idea with me. It comes from Alcoholics Anonymous.

is how it has always been. But I hold my precious little Boaz to my breast, and I cannot forget the children of Jericho. They were precious too.

Sometimes when he sees the sadness in my eyes, Salmon says, "It will be different when the Messiah comes." He tells me that someday God will send his chosen one to bring in the Reign of God. Then there will be no more war and cruelty, no more hunger or injustice, and the whole world will be filled with peace. Salmon says, "The crooked shall be made straight, and the rough places plain" (Isa. 40:4 KJ). I long for the day.

Tell me more about the Messiah, I plead. And Salmon says, "His name shall be called Wonderful, Counsellor, The mighty God, the Everlasting Father, The Prince of Peace" (Isa. 9:6 KJ). I love to say the words over to myself.

I like to think of the Wonderful Counsellor. He will be wiser even than Salmon, whom I love so much. I long to sit at the Counsellor's feet and learn from him. Blessed are the humble, the teachable, for they shall obtain wisdom.

And I visualize this Prince of Peace. He will treat women with respect and courtesy, even harlots. He will gather children in his arms, the Canaanite children and the Hebrew children together. He will carry young lambs gently. He will care about the grass and the flowers. He will give a special place in his kingdom to the poor. He will comfort those who mourn and feed the hungry and thirsty. There will be room in his kingdom for the merciful, the pure-hearted, the peacemakers, and the persecuted.

Meanwhile I try to raise our little Boaz to be gentle and generous and to be concerned about the poor and the strangers. I will teach him to treat women with respect.

And so the generations will go right forward until the Messiah comes and the Kingdom of God is established on earth, as it is in heaven.

# $\mathcal{R}uth$

Background: The Book of Ruth

*. . . your daughter-in-law who loves you, who is more to
you than seven sons . . .[Ruth 4:15].*

My father named me Ruth, and I have loved my name. In my
own language Ruth means Beloved and reminds me that I was
a wanted child, even though a girl. In Hebrew, if you spell it
backwards, it means Turtledove, a symbol of spring and rebirth.
You remember the song:

> For lo, the winter is past, the rain is over and gone,
> The flowers appear on the earth; the time of singing has come,
> and the voice of the turtledove is heard in our land.
> [Song of Sol. 2:11-12]

And I have heard that there is another language in which my
name means Pity or Gentleness. People speak of being ruthless and they mean merciless or cruel. And in that same language, Ruth rhymes with truth. Love, springtime, gentleness,
truth! In a way that is the story of my life.

Moab, my country, lies east of the Dead Sea. The ground is
fertile and there is sufficient rain. Things grow well and life is
good. I never could understand why the Hebrews thought of
the area west of the Dead Sea as a "land flowing with milk and
honey." When it rains enough, there are good wheat and barley
crops, the fig and olive trees yield much fruit, and the grapes
grow large and sweet. Often, however, there is not enough rain
and people are hungry. Their history is full of stories about going to Egypt in times of famine.

It is also strange that my people and the Hebrews think of
themselves as enemies. We speak dialects of the same language,
and we must have come from the same Semitic stock generations back. The Hebrews have no use for our god, however, and
they frown on the fertility rites of the Moabite women. They
think that their God, Yahweh, is the only God in heaven and
earth. And I have come to believe that too.

People are individuals, however, and there has always been
some trade between the Hebrews and Moabites, and friendships

and alliances formed. During a time of famine in Judea, a family from Bethlehem came and settled in our village. Elimelech and Naomi were the parents' names, and they had two young sons, Mahlon and Chilion. They were good people and we were glad to have them as neighbors.

I first saw Naomi at the town well, soon after they arrived. I stood and stared at her. She was the most beautiful woman I had ever seen, with great poise and self-assurance. She asked me to help her draw water from our well. I was at the age when girls get crushes on older women, and I gave her my heart. I have never taken it back. Even now when she is old and frail, she is beautiful and wise. I think she is the most whole person I have ever known.

It is not that I did not love my own mother. But she was like all the other women I knew — burdened and fearful, and gaunt from much child-bearing. My mother was something of a complainer. I had always resented having been born a woman until I met Naomi. She made me proud to be a woman. She did not see work as a burden; she made it enjoyable, and she taught me many practical things. More important, she gave me confidence in my own ideas and my own ability. She said that men may not give women any credit for being intelligent and may treat them as if they own them, but underneath a gentle exterior, a woman can take charge of her own life and use her circumstances to advantage. "Be harmless, like the turtledove," she used to say to me, "but underneath be as wise as a serpent."

Naomi did not have any daughters; I came to play that role in her life even before I married one of her sons. I always hurried through my work so that I could have time to spend at their house. It was a comfortable family to be with, and I liked the boys, as well as Naomi and her husband. They did not tease me like most of the boys I knew, and they would talk to me about things that interested them. I liked Mahlon especially. Sometimes I took my girl friend, Orpah, to be with Naomi. She and Chilion grew to be good friends, and the four of us had many merry times together.

Then Elimelech took sick and died after a brief illness. Mahlon and Chilion now had to assume responsibility for the family. Naomi thought it was time for them to marry, and it seemed inevitable that Orpah and I become their wives. We moved into the household with Naomi and her sons and we were a very happy family. The boys were good husbands, and the only thing that troubled us was that neither Orpah nor I had any children. It was hard to understand why.

Ten years passed quickly. Then a sudden epidemic hit our town. Both Mahlon and Chilion were taken sick and died the same day. Now we three women were left alone. We hoped that somehow we could find a way to stay together, though we knew it would not be easy without a man to support us. It was an anxious time, and we missed our good husbands and continued to mourn for them.

Naomi came back from the well one day very thoughtful. A trader from Judea had been there; she had asked him about conditions there and learned that there were prosperous times now. There had been good growing seasons for several years.

As we ate our supper, Naomi said that she thought she should return to Bethlehem. Her husband must still have property there, and there must be relatives there who would be willing to redeem it and keep it in the family. Women could not own property, but they could hold it in trust for some male relative. Certainly, she reasoned, it would be easier to make her way among her own people than in Moab.

"But what will happen to us?" Orpah and I both cried out.

Naomi was firm: "You must go back to your mother's homes. You are still young. Your families can find good husbands for you."

She assured us she would always treasure the years we had shared and be grateful for the happy years we had had with her sons. "But this time of our lives is over," she said, "and we must look ahead and plan realistically."

We clung together and wept a long time. Then Naomi reminded us that Yahweh is the "father of the fatherless and the protector of the widows" (Ps. 68:5). She was tired and went to bed.

Orpah and I talked in low voices far into the night. How could Naomi make the trip to Bethlehem alone? But even more important, how could we give up our life with her and let her go, knowing we would never see her again? We decided we must go with her.

In the morning Naomi would not hear of it. How could we ever find husbands in Judea? Our only hope, she said, lay here in our own country. Energetically she set out to sell her furniture and household things and the few animals we kept so that she would have money for the journey. She made light the dangers of going alone to Bethlehem. She insisted we must return home and make new lives. We gave up arguing with her and asked if we might walk part way with her before our final good-bye. She agreed, and said that when we reached an old tree that stood out on the horizon, we must turn back.

Meanwhile Orpah and I talked things over with our families. My father had died; I could see that my mother was not looking forward to another mouth to feed, although she assured me that it was still my home and I would always be welcome. She knew of my love for Naomi and said she would not stand in the way of my going.

The next day we set out. Orpah and I had collected a change of clothing, some food, and what money we could scrape together and tied them in our scarves. We did not intend to turn back. Noami set a good pace and we sang as we walked along. When we reached the tree, she said, "May God deal kindly with you, my daughters, as you have dealt with those who are gone and with me. May God grant that you each find a good home in the house of a new husband." She kissed us tenderly and we wept together.

Once again we said we really wanted to go with her. She joked and said, "So you think I can still have sons for you to marry! And even if I had them tomorrow, would you wait for them to grow up?" We all laughed. Orpah then kissed her one last time and turned homeward, but I still could not bring myself to join her. My mind was made up.

I turned to Naomi and said to her from the depths of my heart, "Entreat me not to leave you, or to return from following after you: for where you go, I will go; and where you lodge, I will lodge. Your people shall be my people, and your God my God. Where you die, will I die and there will I be buried. The Lord do so to me, and more also, if anything but death part us" (Ruth 1:16-17 KJ). Naomi held out her hand to me and we walked on together. Our lives would be joined from now on.

Our journey took nearly five days. We carefully rationed the food we had. We slept in the fields by night and kept each other warm. Our road lay northward over the fertile rolling fields of Moab until we came to the southern end of the Jordan River, which we forded near Jericho. Then we turned westward and the land became hot and desolate. It seemed like a long time until we came to the grassy hills of central Judea. Finally on the fifth day, Naomi pointed out in the distance the white-washed houses of Bethlehem on the hillside; we hurried our steps. As we came near the town, we noted that the barley was ready for harvest.

People had seen us coming and ran out to see who the two women traveling alone toward Bethlehem were.

One woman said, "Why, aren't you Naomi, Elimelch's wife?"

She assented and then added, "Do not call me Naomi; call me *Mara*, for the Almighty has dealt bitterly with me."

(*Mara* is a Hebrew word meaning Bitter. Naomi had used an ancient word for God I had not heard her use before. It seemed to emphasize a feeling that God had deserted her.)

I realized that the journey had taken a good deal out of her; God no longer seemed like the "protector of widows." Now that we had finally finished our long journey, she gave way to utter exhaustion.

People were kind. They suggested a place we might rent for very little money. Straw for pallets and food were brought. After we had eaten, Naomi lay down and fell asleep immediately. I was troubled. She had always had such boundless energy. It hurt to see her so discouraged and worn out.

I thought things through. I must take charge of things now and be no burden to her. I would find some way to support us both. I remembered that the barley was ready to harvest. I could glean and provide us with food for our immediate needs, and by the time the harvest was over, there would surely be other possibilities. Having decided on a plan I fell asleep and slept soundly. I woke before dawn, refreshed. I told Naomi of my intentions, and she agreed that my idea was good.

I headed for the fields we had seen on our way into town. I saw some men reaping with sickles; they were followed by women tying stalks into sheaves. I asked one of the men politely if I might glean after them. He gave me permission and I began filling my scarf with the barley left in the rows. It was hard stooping work, and I had not eaten since the night before. I stood up to rest my back, and the tears came. I was so far from home. I thought of my family whom I had left so casually and realized I would probably never see them again.

But I could not waste time in regret. I went back to work.

Presently the owner of the field came. He greeted the reapers with a blessing, "May the Lord be with you," and they responded, "and with you also." Then he saw me and asked, "To whom does this woman belong?" (I smiled to myself. How like a man to assume I must belong to some man! He didn't know that there was no man in my life to whom I could belong.) The reaper told him I was Naomi's Moabite daughter-in-law. Would I always be the Moabite, the outsider?

He turned to me and said kindly, "Do not glean in any other field but this. I will tell my men not to bother you. If you are thirsty, feel free to drink from the water the men have drawn. It is good water; it will quench your thirst."

I could hardly believe his kindness. I fell to my knees and asked, "Why should you take notice of a stranger?"

He told me that he had learned of my devotion to Naomi, and added, "May the God under whose mantle you have taken refuge repay you for all you have done for Naomi."

Then he left. I asked one of the women tying sheaves who he was, and she said his name was Boaz. I was thirsty and found the water delicious. One of the men said it came from the well beside the city gate which was famous for its water. I felt refreshed and returned to gleaning.

At noon Boaz returned and insisted that I eat with him and the others. There was parched grain and bread which we dipped in wine. When I returned to gleaning, I realized Boaz must have told his people to leave more behind for me. By the end of the day I triumphantly took home nearly a bushel to Naomi. Things would be all right. We could take care of ourselves.

Naomi was astonished at the amount I had gleaned and asked where I had worked. I told her about Boaz. "God has not deserted us," she exclaimed, "for this man is a relative of ours." I noted that she said "ours" and not "mine" and I was touched. She said that she had assumed when she returned to Bethlehem that she would have to hope some relative of her husband would marry her and redeem the field, even though she was past the age of child-bearing and so not a desirable wife. But now she realized that Boaz might already be thinking about redeeming the property by marrying me and this would be a better solution to our problems.

Each day I gleaned, and each night I brought home much barley. Naomi was sure Boaz would make some move any time, but nothing happened. I had learned that he was not married, which seemed like a miracle to me. Naomi could not understand why he did not act, but she never gave up hope that he would eventually marry me.

The end of the barley harvest came, and still Boaz had said nothing. Now would come the night when the sheaves were threshed. They would be crushed with heavy mallets, and in the evening when the wind came up, the barley would be winnowed. The crushed sheaves would be tossed into the air so that the wind would blow the chaff away and let the grain fall to the floor. It is always a time of merry-making and celebration.

Naomi had a plan. On the evening of the winnowing I was to bathe and put on my best clothes. I was to go to the place after dark, taking care not to be seen. By then the men would be eating and drinking; in time they would be drowsy. Customarily they slept there all night. I was to watch where Boaz lay down, and when he was asleep, I was to lift the cover and lie down. Then she added with a wink, "He will tell you what to do then." I laughed, and agreed to do what she said.

So I bathed and dressed and slipped through the quiet streets till I came to the threshing floor where Boaz and the men were celebrating. I watched in the shadows a long time. Eventually talk slowed, and one by one the men found places and lay down. Boaz was the last. Fortunately he chose a place at the end of a large pile of grain, some distance from the others, and lay down under a light cover. When I was sure he was sound asleep, I cautiously lifted the blanket and lay down. My heart was pounding, but I kept very still.

It must have been around midnight when he stirred and turned over, half rousing. He was startled to find someone there. Quietly he asked, "Who are you?"

(Oh my dear, dear Boaz! This time you did not say "to whom do you belong?" You spoke to me directly, as a person in my own right!)

I whispered, "I am Ruth, your servant. Spread your mantle over me, for you have the right of redemption over me."

At our first meeting he had spoken of my taking refuge under God's mantle, and now I used the same word, asking for his protection.

His reply astonished me, and moved me to tears.

"May the Lord bless you, my daughter," he said. "You have

made this last kindness greater than the first, for you did not run after young men, rich or poor. And now, do not be afraid, for I will do what you ask."

Dear Boaz! He had assumed I would prefer a younger husband! Somehow he had managed to turn the big thing I was asking of him into a kindness on my part! Was there ever such a kind and gracious man?

He explained to me then that though he was a near relative, there was a closer one who had the first right of redemption. That was why he had said nothing earlier. Before day I slipped quietly home, taking care not to be seen. But before I left, he had given me six measures of the winnowed barley as a gift to Naomi.

I hurried home and slipped quietly into the house, hoping not to wake Naomi. Of course she had been too excited to sleep, and I told her all that had happened. She nodded and said, "He will not rest. He will settle the matter today."

And he did! In the morning he went to the city gate, where business is transacted. Here the caravans come, and merchants spread out wares and bargain with customers. Here the city elders meet to settle disputes and act as judges when need arises.

Boaz waited and presently the kinsman with the prior claim appeared and Boaz motioned him to sit down. Then he summoned ten elders as witnesses. He explained that Naomi had land of her husband Elimelech. Would the kinsman redeem it to keep it in the family? The man said he would. Then Boaz explained that the property entailed a levirate marriage with Naomi's widowed and childless daughter-in-law. Realizing then that the land would eventually go to this daughter-in-law's son, if she had one, and not to the sons he already had, the man decided against it. "Take the right of redemption yourself," he said to Boaz. And to bind the matter, he took off his sandal and gave it to Boaz in the presence of the elders, as was the custom.

The elders said, "We are witnesses." One of them added, "And may Yahweh make the woman coming into your house like Rachel and Leah, who built up the house of Israel. And may your house be like the house of Perez, whom Tamar bore to Judah, because of the children you will have by this young woman."

Then Boaz hurried to tell us all that had happened. We were married, and Naomi and I left our little cottage to live in his large, spacious house. We were no longer poor. And Yahweh did bless us. Our son, Obed, was born within the year.

When the midwife laid him in Naomi's arms, she said, "Blessed be God who has not left you this day without a kinsman, and may his name be renowned in Israel. He shall be to you a restorer of life and a nourisher of your old age. Your daughter-in-law who loves you, and who is more to you than seven sons, has born him." And Naomi smiled and kissed me. "Sons are indeed good to have," she said, "but so are daughters."

The years have been good to me. My Boaz is all that his mother Rahab hoped he would be: gentle, generous, concerned for the poor, kind to strangers, and respectful and courteous to women. He often turns to Naomi and me for advice and makes us feel like partners in his enterprises.

Naomi and I often think of the two widows who set out from Moab, grieving for lost husbands, not knowing what the future might bring. But we were bonded together in love. We had a sense of adventure, facing the unknown together.

I have come to love Bethlehem. It seems to me like a holy city, lying here on the hillside. Boaz tells me that it has been prophesized that some day the Messiah will be born in our little town. I like to think that this may be so.

Someday, when the Messiah comes, there will be neither bond nor free, neither Moabite nor Hebrew, neither male nor female. We will all be one people, members of one another.

Someday, when the Messiah comes, strangers will be taken in, the hungry fed, and the thirsty given drink, whoever they are.

Someday, when the Messiah comes, I think he will be something like my Boaz!

# $\mathcal{B}atḫsḫeba$

Background: II Samuel 11-12; I Kings 1-2

*... and the woman was very beautiful...*[II Samuel 11:12].

I'm Bathsheba. My life has been bound up with King David since before I was born. My grandfather, Ahithophel, was David's chief counsellor (I Chron. 27:33). He helped David plan the strategy that enabled the Israelites to defeat Ammon, Moab, and Edom, stretching the kingdom all the way to the Gulf of Aqaba and the Red Sea, and, incidentally, adding great wealth to the royal treasury.

My father was Eliam, one of the thirty-seven top generals in David's army (II Sam. 11:3, 23:34). My deeply pious father was devoted to David and believed him to be Yahweh's agent in establishing the Children of Israel in the Land of Promise. He considered his oath to David as sacred as his oath to Yahweh. He named me Bathsheba, which means Daughter of the Oath.

I did not see my father often when I was growing up because he was away much of the time on various campaigns to consolidate David's empire. In fact, he was home so seldom that my mother had only one child. Men on campaigns take oaths to remain sacramentally clean until the battle is won. This means, among other things, having no relations with women, even their wives. Even when he was home, my father often did not spend the night with us. My mother and I lived in the camps with the other women and children.

But at last David came to the point where he could say:

> With exultation I will divide up Shechem,
>   and portion out the Vale of Succoth.
> Gilead is mine, Manasseh is mine;
>   Ephraim is my helmet;
>   Judah my scepter.
> Moab is my washbasin;
>   upon Edom I cast my shoe;
>   Over Philistia I shout in triumph.
> Who will bring me to the fortified city?

[Ps. 108:7-10]

Then Jerusalem was captured. David established himself there and built his palace. We stopped being tent dwellers and moved into a nice house in the city.

> Pray for the peace of Jerusalem!
> May they prosper who love you!
> Peace be within your walls,
> And security within your towers!

> [Ps.122:6-7]

Soon after we moved to Jerusalem my mother died, and my father sought to make a suitable marriage for me. He had a friend, Uriah, among the generals in David's army. He was a Hittite and a convert to Judaism. His people had once been a strong empire northeast of Canaan with an advanced civilization. Abraham, the patriarch, found them helpful when he sojourned on the edges of their land. When Sarah died and he needed a place to bury her, his Hittite neighbors told him to take whatever seemed suitable. Abraham, however, insisted on paying Ephron four hundred shekels of silver for a cave he owned (Genesis, chapter 23). Long before I was born, the Hittite empire had broken up and the people scattered.

Uriah was a professional soldier — competent and courageous. He came to see if all he had heard about David was true; finding that it was, he offered him his services. He was willing to convert to Judaism and was given the name Uriah which means Yahweh is Light. He had all the zeal of a new convert. He was upright and completely loyal to David. My father proposed to him that he marry me.

At first I was disappointed. I had hoped for someone young and handsome, but my misgivings were soon laid to rest. Uriah was a wonderful husband. He was flattered to have a young wife, one that people considered beautiful. He loved to take me places and to be seen with me. At home he was thoughtful and unfailingly kind. He found my chatter amusing, and I learned how to make him laugh and to help him relax. He thought up little surprises for me and brought me costly and beautiful gifts. I came to love him devotedly and I missed him very much when he was away.

The men usually were home in Jerusalem during the summer, through the harvest season. They grew restless with the arrival

of the New Year in the fall after the food was gathered in.
David usually planned a campaign then to secure a border or to
add new territory. Each year when Uriah went off I hoped I
would have a child on the way. I wanted so much to give him
sons, but Yahweh did not grant my prayers.

A certain summer passed: the harvest was in and stored, and
the wine was made. Word came to Uriah to be ready in three
days to leave for a drive to take Rabbah, the capital city of
Ammon. I helped get his things in order, and he went for the
ritual cleansing of men going into battle. Sadly we kissed one
another good-bye. We both knew I was not pregnant this year.

A week passed. Jerusalem seemed so empty with only women
and children and old men in the streets. There was little to do
and the weather was terribly hot. My maid suggested that I
take my bath in the open courtyard at the center of our house,
instead of my room. There was a small pool in the court. It was
completely surrounded by a wall, so no one from the street or
neighboring houses could see in. I lingered by the pool. A little
breeze sprang up and the water felt cool. My maid dried me
with a towel and then rubbed me down with oil. I dressed slowly.

I never thought about the King. I had just assumed he was
off with his army. But David had business to finish up and had
tarried behind the others. He too was hot, and when the wind
came up in the afternoon, he went up on the palace roof to
enjoy it — the one place in all Jerusalem that commanded a
view of our courtyard. So, unknown to me, he had watched me
enjoying the pool and the breeze.

I was scarcely dressed before there was an insistent knock at
the door. My maid hurried to open it and was taken aback to
find two of the king's attendants with a message that I must
come at once to the palace. I tried to stifle the panic inside me.
Had something happened to Uriah, or to my father?

I had seen David many times from childhood on, but always
when I was in a crowd, or with my father or grandfather. I was
terrified now to find myself alone with him, for his immediate
presence was overwhelming. His body was still lean and hard
and beautiful. He radiated energy and vitality. His dark eyes
held my gaze, and I found him the most magnetic person I had
ever met. No wonder men gave him their allegiance and were
ready to die for him; no wonder women gave him their hearts
and their bodies.

He lost no time telling me that he had seen me and making clear why he had sent for me. I shrank back and wished the floor would open and swallow me. Noticing my discomfort, he asked gently if he was really so repulsive to me. I had to shake my head.

"Do not be afraid," he said. And without further words he gathered me in his arms and carried me into the room behind us.

I have been blamed so often for what happened. But I ask you, what choice did I have? Women have no rights. Furthermore, he was the King. He had absolute life and death power over his subjects, both men and women.

An hour later, back home, I flung myself on my bed and sobbed. David had more wives and concubines than he could count. I was just one more beautiful woman to him. He used me and then dismissed me. My life would never be the same again.

Anxiously my maid and I counted the days and hoped. Within a few weeks, however, it was apparent that what Uriah had longed for and been denied had been given to David who did not want it. I sent him a terse message: "I am with child." He replied that I should not worry, he would take care of things.

He sent a message to Joab, his commanding general, asking that Uriah return to the palace and report on the campaign. He came and dutifully told David all that was going on down to the last detail.

David thanked him and then said casually, "You've had a long trip, and you have served me faithfully. Take some time off and spend it with your wife."

But Uriah was faithful to his oath. He slept at the palace on the floor with the King's servants, and I did not see him. In a way I was relieved. How could I face him and pretend things were all right?

When David learned that Uriah had spent the night at the palace, he again urged him to go home.

Uriah replied icily: "Is not the Ark of the Covenant lodged in a tent and do not my commander, Joab, and your other generals sleep in the fields with their men? Am I then to go to my house and eat and drink and sleep with my wife? As Yahweh lives, I will not do this thing."

David shrugged and told him to spend the night at the palace and return to the field in the morning. That night David tried to get him drunk so that he could be carried home. But Uriah spent the night on the floor at the palace. I never saw him again.

In the morning David wrote a note to Joab, sealed it with the royal seal, and asked Uriah to deliver it. Joab was to place Uriah in the thick of the next battle and then withdraw support so that he would be killed. Oh my poor upright, faithful Uriah — carrying his own death warrant in obedience to his King! I will mourn him as long as I live.

When the official mourning was ended, David sent for me. The priest performed a ceremony; I became a member of the harem and part of the palace life. Both my father and grandfather were shocked at what had happened, but they said nothing, for they feared David's anger. And once I was married to David, they found it advantageous to have me at court and close to the King. My grandfather helped me learn my way around. David was attentive and solicitous, and for a while I had the reputation of being his favorite. In due time a son was born to us, and David was proud and happy.

But Yahweh was angry. Before long, Nathan, the prophet, came to David and told him a story of a rich man with many flocks, and a poor man with one little lamb whom he dearly loved. The rich man coveted the poor man's lamb and killed him to get it. David was outraged, and declared the man deserved to die.

Then Nathan said to David, "You are the man!"

Nathan prophesied that our small son would die. David was conscience-stricken now and prayed earnestly:

> Have mercy on me, O God, according to thy steadfast love;
> according to thy abundant mercy blot out my transgressions.
> Wash me thoroughly from my iniquity, and cleanse me from
> my sin!
> For I know my transgressions, and my sin is ever before me.
> . . . . . . . . . . . . . . . . . . . . . . . . . . . . . . . . . . . . . . . . . . . . . . . . . . . . . . . . .
> Create in me a clean heart, O God, and put a new and right
> spirit within me.
> Cast me not away from thy presence; and take not thy holy
> Spirit from me.
>
> [Ps. 51:1-3; 10-11]

Our child became ill. David fasted and did penance but his prayers were of no avail. After a week the baby died. David looked at the little body and said, "I shall go to him, but he will not return to me." Then he ordered food and went about his business as usual. My body ached for my child, and I grieved a long time.

Before long, however, I knew I would have another child. When our second son was born, David named him Solomon, which means Peace. The prophet Nathan who had denounced David now came and said that he would add the name Jedidiah, which means Beloved of Yahweh. This was a sign that David was forgiven and that this child would be blessed.

David was overjoyed. He asked what gift he could give me to commemorate this happy birth and our restoration to Yahweh's favor. I told him that I wanted Solomon to be King after him. He readily agreed. It was not a light thing to ask, of course, for David had many older sons with prior claims to the throne. In time I bore David two more sons.

David was a remarkable person. He was a brilliant general, personally courageous, and able to lead his men and command their loyalty. He succeeded in unifying Israel and creating a vast empire. He was also a great statesman, with a vision of a well-run city and country where people could live in prosperity and peace. He made a nation out of a fragmented and scattered nomadic people. He was decisive, and at times, ruthless. He had enormous ambition.

I was troubled by David's ruthlessness and cruelty. Power corrupts, and I feel that life and death power should belong only to Yahweh. My grandfather used to say that the good of a strong, undivided Israel outweighed David's killing of those who stood in his way. He warned me never to criticize David, lest I lose his favor. I learned to keep my thoughts to myself, to be patient and forbearing, and to watch for the right moment to approach David for things I wanted.

With all this, he was also tender and even sentimental. At times his generals feared lest his sentimentality get in the way of completing a campaign or finishing off an adversary. He could be very gentle, and he did thoughtful things for those he loved. He was impetuous. He was not ashamed to cry when moved by emotion.

He was also deeply pious. When he prayed, one felt the presence of Yahweh right there in the room, listening. No one doubted that he and Yahweh spoke together, directly and intimately. He loved his God. One of the most beautiful things I have ever seen was his dancing before the Ark of the Covenant, his wonderful body expressing its joy in the Creator. I think his greatest gift was as a poet. He created many beautiful songs for festivals and worship services. Words and music seemed to flow out of him spontaneously. He had a gift for saying the right thing in beautiful language.

Many stories are told about him. One I loved concerned an early campaign against the Philistines. He and his small band were hard-pressed; David became discouraged. They were hiding out in a cave near Adullam, the city of his ancestor Tamar. They knew they might be ambushed at any moment. David prayed:

> I cry to thee, O lord;
> I say, Thou art my refuge, my portion in the land of the living.
> Give heed to my cry; for I am brought very low!
> Deliver me from my persecutors; for they are too strong for me!
>
> [Ps. 142:5-6]

In his weariness David longed for a drink of water from the well by the gate at Bethlehem — that same well whose water had refreshed his great-grandmother Ruth when she gleaned the field of Boaz. Three of David's men slipped out, and against great odds they passed through the enemy lines to bring back water from the well. David was incredulous and deeply moved by their love and devotion. He could not bring himself to drink the water, but poured it out as an offering to Yahweh, saying, "Far be it from me, O Lord, that I should do this. Shall I drink the blood of the men who went at the risk of their lives?" (II Sam. 23:13-17)

> O God, thou art my God,
> I seek thee, and my soul thirsts for thee;
> My flesh faints for thee,
>    as in a dry and weary land where no water is.
>
> [Ps. 63:1]

Solomon grew tall. He had a lot of David in him. Even as a child he had a royal bearing and commanding presence. Most people loved him. His half-brothers found him amusing when he was small, but they resented him when he grew older. He could out-think them and this was disconcerting. Even as a child, Solomon would say profound things in a deceptively simple way. David used to comment: "The testimony of the Lord is sure, making wise the simple" (Ps. 19:7).

David never dared relax, for he had enemies not only on the borders, but also within the palace. His third son, Absalom, in line for the throne after the deaths of his older brothers, planned a revolt to overthrow David. He went to Hebron and gathered supporters around him. It was a severe blow to David that his own son revolted, and it was a heavy blow to both of us that my grandfather, Ahithophel, David's long-time advisor, joined Absalom. David fled Jerusalem; he preferred to fight in the open and did not want Jerusalem besieged. He lamented:

> Even my bosom friend in whom I trusted,
> who ate of my bread, has lifted his heel against me.
>
> [Ps. 41:9]

In time the rebellion was put down. My grandfather committed suicide; Absalom was killed. David mourned for his son a long time: "O my son Absalom! Would God that I had died for thee." (II Sam. 18:33 KJ).

So the years went by. David was thirty years old when he came to the throne; he ruled forty years. It was sad to see him grow old, to watch the once vigorous, well-disciplined body decline. Finally he took to his bed, and no amount of covers could keep him warm.

> I am poured out like water,
> and all my bones are out of joint;
> my heart is like wax,
> it is melted within my breast;
> my strength is dried up like a potsherd,
> and my tongue cleaves to my jaws;
> Thou dost lay me in the dust of death.
>
> [Ps. 22:14-15]

His men hoped that a young, beautiful woman might stir the old fire; Abishag, a girl of the harem, came. She served him faithfully as a nurse, but she could not restore him to vigor.

Meanwhile people angled for position in the impending succession crisis. Adonijah, the eldest son since Absalom's

death, moved ahead to take over the throne, encouraged by
Joab, David's general. Invitations went out to a great feast at
which it was planned to proclaim Adonijah King. Neither
Nathan nor Solomon received invitations, but Nathan learned
what was going on. He urged me to go at once to David. Abishag
let me in, and I bowed low to David who was propped up in
bed. I reminded him of his promise about Solomon and told
him of the feast Adonijah was planning. Solomon and I would
not be safe if Adonijah came to the throne, I said. David reas-
sured me of his intentions with regard to Solomon, and I
withdrew.

Then Nathan went in, confirmed what I had said, and told
David the feast was to take place that very day. David sent at
once for Zadok, the priest, and Benajah, a general in the army.
He gave them instructions: Solomon was to be seated on
David's own mule, and with Zadok, Nathan, Benajah, and the
King's private body guard, they should proceed at once to the
Spring of Gihon in the Kidron Valley. It was done. There Zadok
annointed Solomon King and placed David's crown on his head.
Benajah blew the trumpet and everyone shouted, "Long live
King Solomon!" Along the return way people took up the
shout. Solomon was popular, and by the time the procession
was back in Jerusalem a large and joyful crowd had gathered.

When Adonijah and his feasting friends first heard the noise,
they assumed the shouts were for him. When his friends realized
that Solomon was already crowned, they quietly slunk away.
Frightened and alone, Adonijah took sanctuary at the Ark of
the Covenant. When Solomon heard that, he went to reassure
Adonijah that if he proved himself worthy he would live safely
in his own house. If he did anything evil, he would surely die.

David sent for Solomon and gave him final instructions, out-
lining who his enemies were and how to deal with them. Then
he turned his face to the wall:

> Hear my prayer, O Lord,
>  and give ear to my cry;
>  hold not thy peace at my tears!
> For I am thy passing guest,
>  a sojourner, like all my fathers.

[Ps. 39:12]

and then the voice rang out clearly:

Yea, though I walk through the valley of the shadow of death,
I will fear no evil, for thou art with me . . .

[Ps. 23:4 KJ]

We buried him in Jerusalem, the city he had rebuilt, the city he loved.

Solomon strengthened his position and made plans to build a temple to house the Ark of the Covenant as a sign that Yahweh would always dwell in Jerusalem. Now my role changed. I was no longer one of many wives, vying for favors. I was the Queen Mother and was treated with great honor. People sought me out to ask favors of the King, and I had to be careful how I let myself be used.

One day Adonijah came to me. I did not trust him, but he assured me that he came in peace. He reminded me that he had expected to be king. He acknowledged that it was the will of Yahweh that Solomon should rule, but he wanted one small favor. He knew Solomon would not refuse me. He said he loved Abishag, the young concubine who had nursed David, and wished to marry her. I agreed to speak to Solomon on his behalf.

Solomon rose when I came in and had a chair brought for me. He said that whatever I asked, he would do. I stated Adonijah's request. I was quite unprepared for his reaction. Sarcastically he said, "Why don't you ask me to give him the Kingdom too!"

He reminded me that the high priest and Joab were still loyal to Adonijah and that the King's harem always goes to the next king, not divided among adversaries. He said, "This shall cost Adonijah his life." He sent for Benajah and ordered him to go and kill Adonijah at once. Then, without another word, he dismissed me.

Back in my room I wept in bitter humiliation. I had hoped my son would be wiser and kinder than his father, but here was the same ruthlessness. One by one he found excuses to kill all Adonijah's supporters and consolidate his rule. Everyone says he will be a strong king, greater even than David, and that Israel will prosper under his rule.

But must a kingdom be built on violence and death? Would it not be possible to build a kingdom on forgiveness and patience, on trust and forbearance? Does God love only the Children of Israel? Does not God love Hittites, members of Uriah's family? Is not the whole human race God's chosen people? I remember the words of one of David's beautiful songs:

103

Thy kingdom is an everlasting kingdom,
  and thy dominion endures throughout all generations.
The Lord is faithful in all his words,
  and gracious in all his deeds.
The Lord upholds all who are falling,
  and raises up all who are bowed down.
The eyes of all look to thee,
  and thou givest them their food in due season.
Thou openest thy hand,
  thou satisfiest the desire of every living thing.
The Lord is just in all his ways,
  and kind in all his doings.
The Lord is near to all who call upon him,
  to all who call upon him in truth.

[Ps. 145:13-18]

So I pray to Yahweh that sometime from the House of David may come a ruler who will reign in such a spirit. I pray for a king who will say, "Love your enemies. Bless those who curse you. Pray for those who abuse you." His Kingdom will be different. It will be God's Kingdom. And he will proclaim, "The Kingdom of God is within you. It is already in your midst."

Then we can go right forward to make of the whole earth a promised land for all God's people.

Even so, come thou son of David. Come, thou son of Solomon. Come, thou child of Bathsheba.